CARNAGE

CARNAGE

NEW WRITING FROM EUROPE

edited by
Michael Blackburn

SUNK ISLAND PUBLISHING

LINCOLN

CARNAGE is issue 6 of *Sunk Island Review*,
published by Sunk Island Publishing, 1992.
Copyright © this collection, Sunk Island Publishing, 1992
Copyright © these translations, the translators, 1992

EDITOR Michael Blackburn
PRODUCTION John Wardle
COVER DESIGN Geoffrey Mark Matthews

The financial assistance
of Eastern Arts Board
and the Arts Council of Great Britain
is gratefully acknowledged.

'Home' by Václav Havel, translated by Paul Wilson,
first appeared in the *New York Review of Books*,
December 1991.

A subscription to *Sunk Island Review* costs £6.50/$20.00
for two issues (i.e. this issue and SIR7) post free.
Add £2.00/$8.00 for overseas postage.
Payment in sterling (or U.S. dollars *cash*) please.

ISSN 0955-9647
ISBN 1 874778 00 0

All submissions (including those from literary agents)
should be accompanied by stamped addressed envelopes
or International Reply Coupons, otherwise they will
not be considered.

SUNK ISLAND PUBLISHING
P.O. Box 74
Lincoln LN1 1QG
England

CONTENTS

A DREAM OF CHURRIANA

María Victoria Atencia
translated by Louis Bourne

I'm seeing the house and myself in her:
Though, bewilderingly, the doors, when closing,
Make my eyelids fall, and her winter nights
Are only my cold feet, and she's flesh of my flesh
Or I'm stone of her, and she's like a little
Nutshell in my pocket, and I'm like a box,
Now empty of tea, in her boat's womb.

But it's my own house, or the one I had,
In which to choose apples that sweetened my mouth
And to walk with my broken doll through the
            hallways
Till the old wardrobe with cathedral doors
That kept the dung for other seedings.

THE FLOOD

María Victoria Atencia
translated by Louis Bourne

The storm put up in the sun's house
And its doors flew open
To a gust of wind blowing me barefoot –
And a girl – to the balcony where I let my feet,
Suspended, hang down.
Below was the gulley riverbed, its sand
Now covered with dirty water and some bodies. The cold
Reached my balcony and, in the current,
Weakened and swept along, a horse stared at me
    before sinking
With Mother's image, a girl, in the broken pupils
    of his eyes.

THIS GAME

María Victoria Atencia
translated by Louis Bourne

Give me a silk bow that will narrow my girth
And bind my waist with the neighbouring back
That's been gathering me for so many years.
My lifelong custom can tell me little
Of what, for better or worse, approaches
My body and grazes it or turns into me myself.

I propose this game: I'll give you something:
Whatever you like. And you give me the slow
Motion to see myself with my things nearby.
Let's stop the shadow of the sun in its dials,
The waters in their rivers. And, just for today,
May the graceful oriole hold back its flight.

ACROSS THERE ON A VISIT

James Brockway

THEY still ask, 'How long have you lived in Holland?' and nowadays, to those I judge to be under forty-six, I reply, 'Longer than you' – though it's not exactly true. I did come back to live in England now and then.

What in the beginning had struck me as inquisitive and rather ill-mannered was actually due to genuine curiosity – a real interest in the world around them. You have to have that interest, if you live in a small country, surrounded by guys bigger than yourself and largely dependent on – and intensely engaged in – international trade.

But a more surprising question, still put, went: 'But why Holland?' Surprising, because although they would vigorously deny it, at heart the Dutch are as chauvinist as any other European nation. Highly critical of others, incorrigibly convinced they know better in all things (for years they have queried or even attempted to correct my English) they nevertheless seemed to think their country was one of the very last places an Englishman would choose to live. So why did I come?

There are always a myriad reasons one does things, most of them unconscious. Only a few weeks ago, and purely by chance, seeing an old 1927 silent film again (I was a film buff at the age of ten), I began to understand the pattern my life has taken and the reason I came to Holland after the war. It had lain pretty deep in my unconscious for forty-six years or more.

But, on the surface of life, the main reasons were: disgust with my work at the Ministry where, after five years of war service, I came back to find them still wrangling about whether this item should be charged to heading

2XB and that to heading 3HY, or whether form 2BZ or 3DY should be used for this, that or the other bit of nonsense. (We were dealing with the supply of artificial limbs to the war wounded.) Disgust with my young fellow students at LSE when I left the Ministry to complete my pre-war university work by full-time study – they were moaning pettishly at slight delays in the payment of their grants when only a year or so before I had seen my pals burned alive in their crashed Beaufighters and when my mate and ex-pilot, Stuart-Cox, had been reported 'missing, believed killed' over Burma. How I despised those puling students. Disgust, too, with life in post-war London, which was chockful of Americans and where I had come home one night to find my room stripped and all my personal belongings removed, because I had complained that morning that the room wasn't being cleaned as arranged. Was this the world we had fought to save from Hitler?

So the second time my friends in Holland wrote asking me to come over and teach English – for five years the Nazis has proscribed all forms of English during their Occupation and the Dutch were crying out for teachers – I decided it wasn't such a crazy idea after all. Though at the Ministry they said: 'You'll lose your pension when you're sixty-five!' (I was twenty-eight) and suggested I saw a psychologist. I was obviously unhinged.

There was, however, a deeper reason, several deeper reasons, why I was attracted to life with my friends in Holland. I won't go into those too much here, though, but merely indicate the situation by saying that, where Christopher Isherwood has written a novel entitled *Down there on a Visit*, I could write another, entitled *Across there on a Visit* – a long, long visit.

I had visited Holland twice at Easter, in 1938 and 1939, and on the second occasion especially I had entered an environment where art in its various forms mattered and was an integral part of life. It was as though I had entered an Aladdin's cave. In England, where despite work at the Ministry during the day and university study in the evenings there had still been time for reading Dostoevsky and D.H. Lawrence, for theatre-going (at sixpence (2½p) a time in the gallery at the Old Vic), cinema-going, art galleries, Sunday afternoon concerts and Sir Henry Wood in person at the Promenade Concerts at the Queen's Hall, art was nevertheless seen as an extra, extraneous to *real* life, something you took an interest in, only if there was time for it. In Holland, I entered homes where you breathed art as a matter of course, took it in with your meat and your wine. It was also a world where English, Dutch, French, German, Italian were spoken and understood and their

11

countries of origin and cultures known and visited. A European world.

To an extent this was due to Holland's being, geographically, a part of the European continent, with the other countries of Europe within easy reach. Even in the early days, a weekend trip to Brussels or into Germany was quite normal. But it was also due to my older Dutch friend's culture and his background and origins. Though Dutch, he was of French extraction and had a French name, with a mother who was half-German and a grandfather (long dead) who had been Governor of the West Indies. The bookshelves were full of international titles and the works of older authors such as Voltaire, Goethe, Heine, Proust.

Despite this general air of culture and the interest in literature, it was not a literary milieu, for my friend was an architect and his father had been a painter. It was mainly due to my own efforts, therefore, that I came to know, vaguely, some Dutch authors – some of them of the older, pre-war generation, and to translate their poetry. I had started writing during the war and my first piece had been accepted by Reginald Moore. So, in Holland, I started writing regularly and placing stories, articles and poems. But I was cut off from the writing world in England and felt this acutely. So when offers of translation work came from academic quarters I allowed it gradually to overtake my own writing, becoming the English translator of a new university institute for many years. My own writing fell off... just a poem now and then in *Outposts*, though I did reach the *TLS* and *The Listener* on occasions.

It was when I moved to Amsterdam ten years later and set up on my own that I also moved closer to the centre of literary life in Holland, though I was never a mixer. Here I began to write about new British authors, people such as Alan Sillitoe, Iris Murdoch, William Golding, for Amsterdam's main paper and set up a series of English novels in Dutch translation at a publisher's, who, although he had both Graham Greene and Angus Wilson on his list, hadn't much more. The idea caught on and was copied by several other Amsterdam publishers. I moved to the *N.R.C.*, Rotterdam-based and Holland's best from the intellectual point of view, and wrote for it on British authors for eight years until it fused with the Amsterdam paper and I was dropped by the new editor.

This inelegant behaviour was, in my experience, not untypical of the Dutch, who can always find you when they need you and just as easily drop you when they don't. By this time I was pretty fully engaged as a reviewer and translator in many fields, particularly in art and literature, giving occasional lectures and working for Dutch World Radio, writing programmes about and interviewing Dutch writers. I had also by now translated the work of several leading Dutch poets and prose writers and knew several of them.

In Amsterdam in my early forties, I lived the youth I had never had, due to Ministry and university work before the war and war-time military service after that. I liked my life in Amsterdam and the simple but romantic attic studio flat a friend let me use at the top of the tallest house along the River Amstel, overlooking the celebrated yellow wooden drawbridge, *de Magere Brug* – a tourist attraction. Piet, the son of one of Amsterdam's wealthiest private bankers, was always complaining that his friends saw him as rich, whereas he was just a poor university lecturer on psychology. His elderly father, he said, would not part with a penny and would not die, either. Ten years later, Piet himself died, as the result of a car accident, predeceasing his father by only three months. So he never inherited. Here, in this family too, you had business combined with art – Piet's father had a celebrated art collection. 'Look,' Piet would whisper in shady hallways of the parental home along the Herengracht, 'Rembrandt – genuine!' Gentle, erudite, witty, Piet was for a few years my lover. A curious relationship. I remain indebted to him for befriending me at the saddest and most difficult moment of my life in Holland.

More than any commissioned work what I enjoyed doing most of all was trying to introduce Dutch prose and poetry that had appealed to me personally into our British literary magazines. In fact the first poem I ever published was a translation from Dutch, done before I left for Holland and really knew Dutch properly. But it was in 1960, when John Lehmann at *London Magazine* took a story I'd done by Maria Dermoût, who wrote about the Dutch East Indies early this century, and a set of poems by a pioneering post-war Dutch poet, Hans Lodeizen, that I began to work more systematically in this way. David Wright took a long Dutch essay for his new magazine X. The *TLS* asked me to review.

I was treated very badly indeed after I had succeeded in getting celebrated Dutch best-seller, Jan Wolkers, introduced in England. The going was not smooth, because, though anxious to break through into the English market, the Dutch do not really like having someone do something for them and succeed. They like to believe they can do everything themselves, although they can't, and some of the reports in the Dutch press about work with which I have have been involved have shown misrepresentation of the facts operating as a fine art.

There were compensations. In 1967, Alan Ross at London Magazine Editions printed my independently-done translation of a fine Dutch novella, *A Day at the Beach* by Heere Heeresma. The project had been turned down as having no future by the government-sponsored Translation Foundation, but, on appearance, the small book got glowing reviews all over the London press and Roman Polanski bought the rights in my version and filmed it, saying it was the best script he had ever written. The film was completed – Peter Sellers had a cameo role in it – but never distributed because of the murder of Polanski's wife, Sharon Tate, and the Charles Manson case.

A few years before, one of the most difficult books I ever translated (difficult for its style), *The Man in the Mirror* by senior Belgian author, Herman Teirlinck, was also very well reviewed in *The Guardian* by Norman Shrapnel, without any mention that it concerned a translation. I was supposed to see this as a compliment. After all, I have always held that the best translator is the invisible translator and here I'd become just that!

Rather than working to commission for the Dutch, who repeatedly sponsored inadequate translations, it was really much more rewarding to translate and place a Dutch story or poem here and there, working on my own, and this I did, choosing the stories and poems myself and seeing it all as my own private game of literary roulette. Sometimes one wins. The first story I mentioned, by Maria Dermoût, which *London Magazine* took in 1960, led to about a dozen further, lucrative placings in New York (in *Harper's Bazaar*).

Back in Holland by 1970, after six years in Cornwall, where I had started writing for *The Guardian* and *Books and Bookmen*, had had more work from the Dutch than when in Amsterdam, and, aided by my Dutch typist in Amsterdam, had also had the cheek to translate Isherwood's novel, *A Single Man*, into Dutch (Isherwood himself was most helpful and forthcoming), I extended my writing in the Dutch papers and literary magazines and much enjoyed contributing to the new, lighter-in-touch Back Page of the *N.R.C.*, helping to establish it as the second most-read page in the newspaper. A new young editor scotched that, as new young editors – sure they know better – do, and the page's reputation has declined.

I was asked to contribute on British authors to a new, young and brash literary monthly, stencilled at first but now, sixteen years later, very smartly produced indeed, which calls itself, unpronounceably, *Bzzlletin*. The publishing house, its name likewise almost unpronounceable, *Bzztoh*, did a volume of my essays and organises literary manifestations in which I have sometimes taken part. But I have never been one for manifestations and conferences and have never, for instance, attended Rotterdam's famous summer get-together, Poetry International, firmly believing that both writing and translating, taken seriously, are very private and personal activities indeed.

During the 'eighties *bezuiniging* (economising, retrenchment) set in, but I still write an article now and then for *Bzzlletin*. Besides continuing my game of literary roulette, in recent years I have concentrated on presenting the work of one of Holland's foremost contemporary poets, Rutger Kopland, in English. I was helped in this by the editor of this magazine, Mike Blackburn, who, while at *Stand*, was the first ever to take and print my translations of Kopland's work, and who later, at Jackson's Arm Press, published the first collection of them, *The Prospect and the River*.

In recent times, again, I've found homes for a few poems by other contemporary Dutch poets, mainly by Tom van Deel and by the doyenne of Dutch women poets who achieved huge sales shortly after the war, Vasalis. Others include Hans Warren, Peter Verstegen, Cees van Hoore, Jos Versteegen, Hans Lodeizen (long dead but still, somehow, contemporary).

I've always felt something missing in working with the Dutch – the elegant, spontaneous, generous gesture seems to be beyond the reach of most of them, and charm simply beyond their comprehension or dignity. I can't be bothered to find out which – anyway they lack charm. But, with one or two exceptions, the individual authors I have known, and still know, are nice enough and often seem to think of the world they work in as I do. Not much.

In my experience, the 'official' world of Dutch writing shows a talent amounting to sheer genius for often preferring the mediocre to the genuine and promoting it with a great deal of ballyhoo. This, I believe, is why Dutch writing never achieves what it could achieve in a healthier climate. How much of this applies to us, I wonder?

AMONG BOXES OF BUTTONS

Bo Carpelan
translated by Anne Born

Among boxes of buttons, broken syllables, words
on the clothesline, among rows of old shoes
in shabby cupboards reeking of mothballs,
amidst all the rubbish, all that's built up
in clay fields or in ditches, suddenly
in some lonely hour you come upon
a great unfamiliar peace.
You recall a tree with a shady crown
that stood outside the window, it said: 'trust me,
listen, and if you are thirsty
the spring from which I drink is infinite, my root
goes so deep into the earth I have almost forgotten it –
the leaves gleam, the years are filled with song.
What more do you want? Have you forgotten me,
I who once offered your childhood shade?'

IT'S HIGH TIME TO AGE

Bo Carpelan
translated by Anne Born

It's high time to age. Others, younger,
behave with dignity, hold wise opinions.
I regard them with amazement and some envy,
the assurance, the clothes, careful attention to health
and the smile that's practised like a lecture.
How trim and neat they are,
well spoken of as horses, and, in the small hours,
with horses' wild eyes. It's high time
to be elected to some order and once a week
have lunch with the likeminded and be dead.

THE TRAIN COMES BACK

Bo Carpelan
translated by Anne Born

The train comes back
to the station
but those taking it
have aged.
They go on their way
as if they were not there.
Their luggage is abandoned
in rusty wagons.
Under the station arches
fly birds
like flakes of soot
in a smoke of white clouds.
A child stands there
with your features
and looks up at you
and the closed windows.

A SITE NEAR BABYLON

Adam Czerniawski
translated by the author

On the third day the mound on the hill revealed the first secret: two roughly-hewn ploughshares. Seven inches lower we dug up a splintered jar. Six days we chipped at a passionless granite vein. Then on Saturday at sun-set we marvelled at the deformed skeleton of a winged unicorn; nearby we found bronze helmets, gold rings, tablets listing the royal fortune and brass statuettes of the fertility goddess Tamir.

Below this nineteen-foot layer of rubbish, tightly wrapped in corrugated cardboard, lay a fractured philosopher's stone.

HE FEELS THE NEED

Jean Daive
translated by Martin Sorrell

He feels the need
to see her
almost naked
sweep
to surprise
around laces
her ripening
nature.

The woman in love
sweeping
reluctant to grow more
whispers
entwines him.

Weaving dance figures
she slips
on linoleum
inlaid
with attractive rings.

Smiles. Hands close
over hands.

She gets to grips with imperfection.

SPRINGTIME BEHIND THE SLAUGHTERHOUSE

Andres Ehin
translated by Richard Caddel and the author

Silence in the slaughterhouse.
No killing going on.
The cleaned-up hooks and rails without
a single joint thereon.

Behind the silent slaughterhouse
I hear the nightingales sing.
Alone, the only meathead
by the birdcherries in spring.

In Estonian, to 'send someone to listen to nightingales' means to kill them.

UNCLE WAS FOUND

Andres Ehin
translated by Richard Caddel and the author

uncle was found in a wardrobe
a coffeecup by the handle in his teeth
a pained look in his old eyes
he staggered downstairs
his forehead wizened
passersby blew smoke in his face
the northeasterly ruffled his grey hair
he walked like a tiny god
a slo-mo god
coffeecup handle between his lips
pained look in his old eyes

just now we found him in a wardrobe

AT EASE

Gabriel Ferrater
translated by Arthur Terry

She is asleep. At this hour
men are already awake, though as yet
only a little light strikes in to them.
A little suffices us: the awareness,
merely, of two things:
the earth revolves, and women sleep.
Assenting, we travel on
to the end of the world. We need
do nothing to assist it.

A SMALL WAR

Gabriel Ferrater
translated by Arthur Terry

They were carrying antitank mines,
heavy and useless, like historic symbols,
covered in blankets thick with the timeless smell
of herbs and mule sweat. Also machine guns
and Stens made in England.
In twos and threes, at straggling intervals,
minute and diligent as lice on a fallen tree,
the Maquis were crossing the Pyrenees.
It was one of the smallest wars we have ever known.
Only a single body came my way, that of
a country girl from Aragon, who got a lift
in an army truck, and became another
obvious symbol. The driver and mechanic
were careless, and the three of them went through a bridge.
The girl had a simple lesion, nothing of interest,
but the doctors who did the post-mortem
found on one ankle a remarkable growth
of hereditary origin, rooted deep in the tree of her race.
And a moment's pain, and the pleasure before it,
seemed small when compared with that defect of centuries,
working in silence. Nothing personal, mind.
It was a war, though a small one.

And, though it was strange, there was nothing personal,
       either,
in the shock that I felt for a moment during the inquest,
feeling the sun beat down on the shed by the wall,
on the tangled stubble of crosses and bones
in that village cemetery, where the stench of death
smelt like an unwashed crotch.
It just meant I was young, like most who go to wars,
who are scared of the flesh, and destroy and abuse it.
All, in a word, emblematic, eternal.

TIME WAS

Gabriel Ferrater
translated by Arthur Terry

Let me escape into your old domain.
Our ghosts still drift about the usual place.
I see the winter sky, the metal footbridge
with its blackened struts, the scurf of grass
along the burnt-up track. I hear the express whistle.
Its gathering thunder rocks the ground we stand on
till we have to shout. We watch it pass.
Your soundless laughter sets me laughing too.
I see your dove-grey blouse, the blue
of your short flared skirt, the red scarf bunched
around your neck, the one I used to call
your country's flag.
All's as it was that day. The words we said
come back, and now, the one bad moment.
Something has silenced us. You've hurt your hand.
Remember how it fluttered and hung limp,
nervously fingering your cycle-bell.
It's just as well we're interrupted.
Now, as before, the tramp of metal heels,
the outsize chant of men in battle dress,
steel-helmeted, surrounds us. A command
darts out like the savage glitter of a snake,
and we hide our faces in the lap of fear
till they have passed. Now we've forgotten

how we were: their unreflecting movement
restores us to ourselves, and we are glad
to be together in this place, not caring if we speak.
So we may kiss. We're young: those distant silences
have no authority;
the fear of others kills our private fears.
Freewheeling down the avenue, we feel the cold
as each tree spreads its heavy mass of shade.
We glide from chill to chill, unconsciously.

FONTAINE DE MEDICIS

Undine Gruenter
translated by *Michael Hulse*

O make me a mask
Dylan Thomas

I CAN see her smile as she sits down on an iron bench in the park where I have been waiting for her. The park will be deserted because she will not come until shortly before the gates are closed. Only a few late idlers will still be sitting along the paths, scattered, with a book, a newspaper, an attache case on their knees. But in the side path of the Fontaine de Médicis, where we are, there will be no one.

A smile, somewhat uncertain, as she bows her head and averts her face. I shall reach out my hand. I shall lean across to her.

It will be evening, by the water, in one of the park's lateral avenues. She, beside me on the bench, will gaze silently at the reflections in the water. The jet of water will already have been turned off. Maybe the toy boat I saw the last few evenings will still be drifting on the water, capsized, aimless. Coming from the warmth of the streets, she will shiver a little in the shade under the trees. She will point to the boat, and laugh. She will say, we've made it today, saved.

Evening at last. I leave my room. I set out on the long walk to the Luxembourg. Rue de la Gaité, Rue Delambre. At this time it is quiet here, no longer day, not yet night. The garages and workshops are already shut, the night clubs not yet open. At the edge of the pavement, a cardboard box or so, with the day's litter. Hotel Mistral, the Résistance meeting place during the German occupation. The Vavin junction is congested as it is every day at this hour. The cars are wedged in amidst each other, there is no way forward or back. The jam reaches far back into the side-streets. People are starting to sound their horns now, inconsiderately, impatiently.

I cross the Boulevard Montparnasse and enter the Sélect. There is enough time for a drink, standing up.

The first time I saw her, she was on her own. In a photographic gallery, without any companion, that was the start of it. Later she was standing amongst a group of friends. The gallery rooms, on the first floor of a house in the Rue Christine, were overcrowded. I went to and fro, circling her. I observed the group in which she stood, a picture I was excluded from.
Then I realised that she was looking across to me, repeatedly, between the heads of those about her. Later she parted from the group she was in and came over to me. She said, you must be Jean's friend. For the first time I heard her voice.

I had met Jean years before when I was studying in Paris for some time on a scholarship. At that time we went to the cinema together now and then. Usually to a small, shabby cinema in a cellar in the Quartier Latin, where they showed *Série Noire* Films. Afterwards we strolled along the streets for a while together, and had a drink at the bar of some café.

I had returned to Germany and we had lost touch. Not long ago I had met Jean again by chance. I had another scholarship, for a year, and a room in Montparnasse, in the Rue Fermat. One Sunday a few weeks ago I had gone to the cinema, and was just leaving when we bumped into each other. It had been a bad film, I was depressed, and that afternoon it was raining.

He invited me to go home with him, so I went to his place, a spacious flat in the Rue du Bac. Most of the rooms looked as if he rarely went into them. Only the study, at the rear of the apartment, looked as if a man possessed lived there. Everywhere there were stacks of blueprints, elevations, architectural drawings. He shoved a pile of drawings off an armchair, the sole place where a visitor could sit down. I sank into the chair, we smoked and drank cognac. We knocked the ash off our cigarettes, and there were long silences. Finally only he was talking. He told me about the woman he was living with, a photographer. She often worked abroad, currently in Berlin. He talked about her and seemed to be missing her a lot.

In the weeks that followed I called again. I learned everyday things, details which, seemingly of no importance, exposed her to me. At first it was no more than curiosity. Then my thoughts began to dwell upon the absent woman.

That evening I walked her home from the photo exhibition. Striding out quickly, her coat flapping, she walked beside me. A short distance, along the Seine *quais*. The evening rush was over, the streets were empty. She walked rapidly and in silence, I saw her face only from the side. At the front door she said goodbye with a smile, saying she still had work to do.

I walked aimlessly about for hours, as night thickened. I hurried through the streets, in a circle, or zig-zagging. In the same city, beneath the same sky beneath which she slept. The night air acquired a bite, but I took no notice of the cold, nor of the wind that blew across the broad embankments of the Seine and through my clothing. The state I was in that night was to be my state in so many nights to come. I hurried through the streets, circling her house.

A few days later she sent me a book of stories. I turned the pages, expecting some hidden message. Here and there I started to read and read on. The passages all dealt with the same recurring motif: hopeless longing.

On the morning when I received the book, I thought the decision had been taken. It was still not yet nine. The postman had woken me when he rang the bell, the bed was still unmade. The only thing it was possible to believe was that the book signalled my wishes were vain.

I placed the book on the kitchen cupboard and did not touch it again. At last I reflected, one disappointment more or less, one woman more or less, what difference does it make? Then came the day I have marked in my notebook. A day in June. I was standing in the kitchen. The kitchen faces on to one of the cramped backyards of Paris, with the windowless rear wall of a hospital opposite. I lived on one of the higher floors, and the last sunlight was aflame on the balcony door. Further below, the pigeons flapped from window to window in the narrow shaft. I stood at the table, registering the cooing and the abrupt flapping of the pigeons' wings, and gazed at the wall opposite. I had gone into the kitchen to pour myself a glass of wine. One of the hottest evenings of the year. Further down a door slammed. A voice shouted. Somebody was fetching in washing from the line outside the shaft window. Without thinking, more by chance, I picked the book up off the kitchen cupboard again. Taking up my glass to have a drink. Till the moment when, turning the pages, I stopped. The sound of cooing and flapping suddenly ceased, as if the shaft were holding its breath. Amidst the pages of the book it had been waiting for me. The sign. From the page, barely visible yet not to be missed, faintly underlined, a single sentence stared up at me. '*To go on, unwavering, to terror,*' he said, '*that is love.*'

I was alone in the flat, which was the sole witness of my longing. I called out her name – whether aloud or softly, I do not know.

The most difficult thing was to interpret the signs. Now, leaving the Sélect and turning into the Boulevard Raspail, I tell myself that I may have interpreted the signs wrongly. But in half an hour I shall know for certain.

That evening in the kitchen I had rushed to the telephone. How to account for my silence? The receiver remained uncommunicative, I could not get her. I spent the evening by the phone. Night fell. I sat there, the receiver in my hand. Not a sound in the night, only the ringing tone of the phone.

The week after, when she invited me round to their place, she was completely calm. She could not possibly have mustered that composure, I thought, if she had made any kind of confession to me. I watched her go round refilling glasses, talking. Jean, as always, remained hidden away in the back room. Her face was totally expressionless. Doubts came upon me. I hoped she was putting on an innocent act. Nothing could have bonded us more firmly than a lie on her part.

In the months that followed I tried to meet her alone, just once. I went to pick her up from her studio in the Rue de Lille. On a pretext, I called on her at home, at a time when Jean was away. But whenever I met her she was in the company of others. Her behaviour was friendly and reserved. I remembered her gaze that first evening, and waited.

I thought, perhaps she is avoiding a *tête à tête*. Were circumstances to blame? Adverse circumstances can sometimes become the very opposite, and make hidden feelings all the more powerful.

A broad gap that could not be closed yawned between the reality and the desire. I went in pursuit of signs. For she sent me postcards, which I kept in a box of their own and looked at time and again. She lent me books and records of old pre-war tangos. *If everything is an exception*, I thought. There could be a hidden meaning in anything, and every hint misinterpreted could become a trap for me.

But there was no development. The plot revolved in a circle.

I sat at home, working, waiting. I wrote letters that piled up on the windowsill and crumbled to dust in the sun. I wrote at night when the wind rose and chased about the dark city. I wrote about the room where I awaited her. Which, lying fallow in the heat, was fading at the edges like a yellowed photograph. I wrote of the evening when she made her way through the crowd to me.

You will have forgotten, but that evening we talked about a new play. A play that everyone was talking about. It was a story of longing, a defence of wishes. There the play was, between us, mantled in our talk. That talk about a third person's text was the bond that joined us. Now, in the isolation of night, I see that whenever one begins to speak it is always in the hallowed body of a third person. In another's text, in a hollow body that fills with new desire.

I believe that at some point I stopped thinking about happiness. Everywhere people are ceaselessly talking about happiness. How important it is to be happy. Everywhere people are making great efforts to appear happy. In reality there is no one who really is. People are busy, indifferent, just as I was.

Some time before four in the morning the wind dropped. The night lightened. Time to go to bed at last. But I listened to the first of the city sounds. I thought of her sleep, of the house where she was sleeping, of the day ahead.

Nothing easier, I told myself, than for two people to arrange a meeting in a huge city. A meeting unobserved by those who knew us, protected by the machinery of the big city.

I considered the room I was sitting in. Just in case she should suddenly be at the door, I started to tidy up.

But perhaps she would decline to come to my place and prefer to go out to a suburb. We could rent a room for the afternoon, as hundreds of other couples do. No one would bat an eyelid.

The nights were simpler. I wrote, and was able to imagine that time was not passing in vain. But by day I sat around waiting for news. I left the flat only when it was unavoidable. Urgent errands, food, laundry.

There were days too when, bathed in sweat and exhausted from having sat awake all night, I welcomed morning and gave up hope. I went to bed and slept all day, and when I looked I realised that dust and disorder were beginning to reclaim the room.

The water's surface will lie smooth as a mirror before our eyes. A dream landscape filled with algae, from which things free of the law of gravity stare at us, motionless. The bars, the head of the Triton, the avenue lined with statues. The vacant benches on wooden legs. Between them, areas of amassed darkness – the foliage of late summer on the trees. And reflections of the clouds, bright expanses in the sky.

In her hand, instead of flowers, there will be a bunch of leaves. I shall collect it from the bushes. A first coolness below the trees, heralding the approach of night. The scent of leaves and earth, different from the daytime scent. It is a scent of shade, rising from the ground as soon as the sun has quit the lawns and the sandy paths amidst the flower beds.

Without knowing it I have crossed the road. I walk along the road that runs round the park. Beyond the bars the paths run straight as a die. They lead into the depths of the park. Already they are deserted and in shadow.

A territory sealed off in the middle of the city. A defined, imaginary location, as if created for meetings. The park – behind the bars. When I had already ceased to expect anything, the words came softly from her lips: *Fontaine de Médicis, in the evening, just before they close.*

Again and again I make the mistake of beginning the story that evening in the Rue Christine. In reality it all began much earlier. The start is here, between the Rue de Vaugirard, which I am just turning in to, and the Place St. Sulpice.

Familiar territory, where I used to live. I had just arrived from Germany on my scholarship. The window of my room was entirely filled with the cupola of the church. A mass of domed, white stone.

Every day I went from the Place St.-Sulpice to the Luxembourg gardens through the short Rue Férou. It is a narrow street with smooth, white-painted walls. Behind the walls are yards where acacias grow and, closed off from public view, old town villas in protected silence.

One afternoon, by chance rather than intent, I went into a small, unprepossessing bookshop on the corner. The cramped space was crammed full of books on the history of photography. From those that had been so well read they were falling apart to those with pages still uncut, the precious picture books and dusty unsaleables, long out of print, were stacked ceiling-high on the shelves. No one disturbed me. I picked up this book or that. I leafed through old shots of the Paris suburbs. A Pomeranian, a concierge wearing a crocheted shawl, a birdcage in a window. An oilcloth on the kitchen table, an open wine bottle, a saucepan on the stove. Then: a deserted suburban street in the first light of dawn. A cloudy sky, rain on the cobbles. A soot-blackened tenement block. On the ground floor a café, closed. A car is parked half on the pavement, a pre-war model with a high, angular body, small windows, and a spare tyre fixed outside on the hatch of the boot. Crossing the street, their backs to us, go a couple. The woman – a bird of paradise in flight above the dreary grey of the street. Dressed in radiant white. She is wearing a wedding gown that reaches to the cobbles. She is looking back over her shoulder. She is looking out of the picture. At some distance from the couple, also seen from behind, is a third person. He is moving in the same direction as the couple.

A page or so further on, a snapshot. A group picnicking on the banks of the Seine. Sitting on the grass in a wide circle with a tablecloth spread out. A busy group, occupied with plates, wine bottles, putting out cheese, white bread, chicken and grapes. A group of people gesticulating in lively fashion. In the foreground a young woman. Her back to the others, she is sitting a little apart. She is the only one looking out of the photograph, her gaze even and straight. A calm face. A collected gaze. It is the same face as that of the bride in the suburban street.

That evening in the gallery I had recognised the face.

I became almost bereft of memory. I became isolated, alone with my sole passion. June came, and August, a summer of unbearable heat. Beneath my soles the first dry leaves rustled, the leafage was withering as early as the beginning of August, and with the process everything seemed to have been obliterated but the thought of her.

I dreamt of the photographs. In the dawn light she is walking along the wet street. The way she walks is slow and wary. The road stretches out under her tread. The silence of the dream is broken by the rustling of the stiff fabric of her long gown. She walks, moving away from me, her back to me. I wait for her to turn, for her face to appear, for her to look at me.

I dreamt that I showed her the photographs. I held them to her face like a mirror. I dreamt that I said to her, *the dream appears in the mirror.*

The Odeon theatre is still shut and makes a deserted and somewhat dusty impression in the late light at the end of this summer's day. Only a few weeks ago they crowded up the steps to the box office and queued for the last remaining tickets, but now there is no one.

Often I have crossed this square shortly before a show began, as the audience were vanishing beyond the doors and the old-fashioned jangle of a bell sounded softly from the foyer across the deserted square.

In the show-cases under the arcades the playbills of the past season were still pinned up, bleached by the sun and starting to come off the wall.

One day I received a further sign. I had already begun to come away from the background of the life I had led hitherto, like a playbill from a wall. With increasing frequency a scrap of recollection – of one of her looks or gestures – would suddenly overwhelm me, and interrupt what I was doing.

You know, she wrote, *perhaps love is nothing but a labyrinth of desires in which one is lost. A delirium of the imagination. For that reason, these stops and falterings, during which memory renders me incapable of doing anything but think of you, are the nodal points in the history of love. They are phases of breakdown, of amnesia. They are periods of time immeasurable in extent, regardless of whether they are short or long, and in them we are lost.*

It was evening, I went about the flat and cleared the table where I had just eaten with a friend who had called by to see me.

The telephone rang. I raised the receiver to my ear. No one to be heard. No one saying anything.

I shouted into the mouthpiece, waited for a reply, the receiver at my ear. At first only a faint crackle had been audible, and then a soughing in the wire like a current of wind.

But with the clearsightedness of love, which imagined it discovered traces of her in even the remotest signs, I was sure. I was relying on an inner certainty which did not tally with any external cause, and I ignored the gaps between the signs. I was convinced that this was the message I had been waiting for.

The silence at the end of the wire was repeated, always at the same time of evening. Every call confirmed my fever. I began to wait for the call. She could not be reached, yet her presence was stronger than anyone else's in my actual acquaintance. After a while, though, my response to the ringing of the phone became part fright and part compulsion, no more. Nothing could be more tormenting than that silent proximity at my ear. It was a proximity that demanded words be spoken at last. It was a silence that prohibited speech. I wrote, *love must be spoken. It exists in language or else it does not exist at all. Only when it is uttered does it become real. Beyond the mute language of the body, it must express itself in words.*

The ringing of the phone became a sign without meaning, as if some anonymous service were fulfilling an order. At first I had supposed I perceived in the repetition the hallmark of the same longing that was consuming me. But the calls led to nothing and became an empty repetition.

I leave the Odeon theatre behind and turn into the smart Rue de Médicis. On the ground floors of some of the blocks facing the Jardin du Luxembourg there are bookshops. In the windows, old engravings of cities, maps, books on theatre history, and Chinese masks are on show. At the corner is the Rostand, where I often went for breakfast at the time I had my first scholarship.

It was quite a big party, one summer evening in the Rue du Bac. The night was yet young, but the rooms already smelled of alcohol and cigarettes. A hazy scene, impregnated with smoke.

I was standing with another guest in the glass french windows, which were open on to the garden. I was only half aware of the conversation behind me. Some minutes later I suddenly understood what I had been hearing. A commission, next week, in Lyon: that much I grasped. The remark was as vague, to me, as the soughing in the telephone wire. But I was immediately convinced that that was my cue. For the day I had registered was also the very day when I too would be in Lyon. I had been invited to lecture, and the trip had been fixed long since.

A week later, towards evening, I was approaching Lyon. Repairs to the track delayed my arrival by an hour. I had not been able to find out where she was staying in Lyon, so I had mentioned the venue and time of my own lecture. Throughout the train journey I had been anticipating nothing so eagerly as the moment when I would locate her in the audience.

At the hotel I just had enough time to unpack my shaving kit. Through a vent in the ceiling, faint daylight entered the bathroom. More clearly than anything else that evening I recall the moment when I put out the shaving-brush, toothbrush and comb in front of the mirror. The tiled walls, the grubby white of the tub, the rust-brown rim round the plug-hole – all of it drove out my dream.

What had I been imagining? I think I had dreamt of a journey that she would accept unconditionally. It was a dream in the style of an operatic film: we would strike out, burning our bridges behind us.

The lecture theatre was far too big, only a few people had come to listen and sat scattered in the rising rows of seats, yawning vacancy between them. The last rays of sunlight entered at a window. I read without knowing what I was reading out. It was purely mechanical speech, divorced from the speaker. I saw faces in the rows, and a microphone positioned beside the lectern.

Night fell, and she had not come.

It is a few minutes to seven, I am almost there, at my goal. There is the fountain where the avenues cross, below the Panthéon. The rush hour traffic has already dwindled. The jet of water sprays into the rays of sun falling at a low angle. I walk along the avenue towards the Palais, then down the steps, and turn right. There are patches scorched bald in the lawns in front of the Palais, but under the trees it is shady.

I spent three days locked in to my flat. On the fourth day the phone rang. I picked up the receiver and the silence hit me like a blow.

Everything started over again: the ringing of the telephone, the silence, my waiting for the next call. Someone or other had me in the palm of their hand, and knew I could not abandon my hope and would blindly obey any sign at all if I suspected the woman it came from was her in the Rue du Bac.

Then I started to go out again. And then it happened again, and I caught a throw-away remark in a chance meeting on the street. She was with two men whom I knew slightly from a time when I was invited to her home. She talked without pause, laughing, and I was not listening properly. I looked at her and heard her laugh. And then she must have said *sotto voce: Thursday evening at seven, Fontaine de Médicis*. She must have spoken very faintly, or else it was the wind, for I could hardly make the words out. I could not say if she had looked at me as she spoke or not. But she was gazing in my direction.

HOME

Václav Havel
translated by Paul Wilson

*This speech was delivered 26th October 1991,
when President Havel·received an honorary degree
at Lehigh University in Bethlehem, Pennsylvania, U.S.A.*

It is a great pleasure for me to receive an honorary doctorate in a town in which many of my countrymen took refuge centuries ago, and which is still the domicile of many Czechs and Slovaks who have found a new home here while retaining close ties, in their minds, to their former country. Their old home is now at an historical cross-roads: it is not only seeking a new form of statehood but, having freed itself from its position as a satellite, it is looking for a new political home both in Europe and globally as well. These two circumstances have led me to share with you some thoughts I wrote down recently on the subject of home.

The category of home belongs to what modern philosophers call the 'natural world'. (The Czech philosopher Jan Patočka analysed this notion before the Second World War.) For everyone, home is a basic existential experience. What a person perceives as his home (in the philosophical sense of the word) can be compared to a set of concentric circles, with his 'I' at the centre. My home is the room I live in for a time, the room I've grown accustomed to, and which, in a manner of speaking, I have covered with my own invisible lining. I recall, for instance, that even my prison cell was, in a sense, my home, and I felt very put out whenever I was suddenly required to move to another. The new cell may have been exactly the same as the old one, perhaps even better, but I always experienced it as alien and unfriendly. I felt uprooted and surrounded by strangeness, and it would take me some time to get used to it, to stop missing the previous cell, to make myself at home.

My home is the house I live in, the village or town where I was born or where I spend most of my time. My home is my family, the world of my friends, the social and intellectual milieu in which I live, my profession, my company, my work place. My home, obviously, is also the country I live in, the language I speak, and the intellectual and spiritual climate of my country expressed in the language spoken there. The Czech language, the Czech way of perceiving the world, Czech historical experience, the Czech modes of courage and cowardice, Czech humour – all of these are inseparable from that circle of my home. My home is therefore my Czechness, my nationality, and I see no reason at all why I shouldn't embrace it, since it is as essential a part of me as, for instance, my masculinity, another aspect of my home. My home, of course, is not only my Czechness, it is also my Czechoslovakness, which means my citizenship. Ultimately, my home is Europe and my Europeanness and – finally – it is this planet and its present civilisation and, understandably, the whole world. But that is not all: my home is also my education, my upbringing, my habits, the social milieu I live in and claim as my own. And if I belonged to a political party, that would indisputably be my home as well.

I think that every circle, every aspect of the human home, has to be given its due. It makes no sense to deny or forcibly exclude any one one aspect for the sake of another; none should be regarded as less important or inferior. They are part of our natural world, and a properly organised society has to respect them all and give them all the chance to attain fulfilment. This is the only way that room can be made for people to realise themselves freely as human beings, to exercise their identity. All the circles of our home, indeed our whole natural world, are an inseparable part of us and a medium of our human identity. Completely deprived of all the aspects of his home, man would be deprived of himself, of his humanity.

I am in favour of a political system based on the citizen, and recognising all his fundamental civil and human rights in their universal validity, and equally applied: that is, no member of a single race, a single nation, a single sex, or a single religion may be endowed with basic rights that are any different from anyone else's. In other words, I am in favour of what is called a civic society.

Today this civic principle is sometimes presented as if it stood in opposition to the principle of national affiliation, creating the impression that it ignores or suppresses the aspect of our home represented by our nationality. This is a crude misunderstanding of that principle. On the contrary, I support the civic principle because it represents the best way for individuals to realise themselves, to fulfill their identity in all the circles of their home, to enjoy everything that belongs to their natural world, not just some aspects of it. To establish a state on any other principle than the civic principle – on the principle of ideology, of nationality or religion for instance – means making one aspect of our home superior to all the others, and thus reduces us as people, reduces our natural world. And that hardly ever leads to anything good. Most wars and revolutions, for example, came about because of this one dimensional conception of the state. A state based on citizenship, one that respects people and all aspects of their natural world, will be a basically peaceable and humane state.

I certainly do not want, therefore, to suppress the national dimension of a person's identity, or to deny it, or refuse to acknowledge its legitimacy and its right to full self-realisation. I merely reject the kind of political notions that attempt, in the name of nationality, to suppress other aspects of the human home, other aspects of humanity, and human rights. And it seems to me that a civic society, the kind that modern democratic states are gradually establishing, is precisely the kind of society that gives room to people right across the spectrum of what determines their nature – all those levels of the natural world that constitute their identity.

A civic society, based on the universality of human rights, best enables us to realise ourselves as everything we are – not only members of our nation, but members of our family, our community, our region, our church, our professional association, our political party, our country, our supranational communities – and to be all of this because society treats us chiefly as members of the human race, that is, as people, as particular human beings whose individuality finds its primary, most natural and, at the same time, most universal expression in our status as citizens, in citizenship in the broadest and deepest sense of that word.

The sovereignty of the community, the region, the nation, the state – any higher sovereignty, in fact – makes sense only if it is derived from the one genuine sovereignty, that is, from human sovereignty, which finds its political expression in civic sovereignty.

Czechoslovakia is now faced with the task of building again, after more that forty years of totalitarian rule, the foundations of a civic society. Such foundations were laid in the United States of America over two hundred years ago, and civic society has been under construction in this country, without interruption, ever since.

It is clear in this situation who can learn more from whom: it is we who can learn from you. Next year has been proclaimed Education Year in

Czechoslovakia, among other things because we will be celebrating the four hundredth anniversary of our own Jan Amos Komenský – Comenius – the great teacher of nations.

I would like to end with a request – the request that you, American scholars, come to our country as often possible and teach us about civic society, about the kind of legislation and institutions it requires, and about what relationships should exist between these institutions and the citizens, and among the citizens themselves.

In short, I hope that you may come to teach us how to build a decent, humane home for all citizens. Thank you.

ODYSSEUS IN BARCELONA

José Hierro
translated by Louis Bourne

If only I'd never returned!
How much better if I hadn't!

Nausicaas and Penelopes
Sailed with me.
I wore them tattooed on my arms
To have them always in sight
And never to forget them.
But my skin's grown wrinkled,
And the divinely young women
Now look like old ladies.
If only I'd never returned!

I arrived with my ears plugged
To be no slave to the spell
Of that song I never managed to hear,
And I found Gothic cypresses,
Stones and beings never dreamed,
Different words.
My islands were not around,
Or maybe they were just a dream.

If only I'd never returned! But I have,
And here I am again,
Caressing this handful of smoke.

LATVIAN LESSONS

Mirela Ivanova
translated by Ewald Osers

– Is this a hotel?
– Yes, this is a hotel. No this is not a hotel.

    Hotels, a sudden home and a strange cosiness,
    asylum for your escapes, a safe abyss.
    Here you always return to, the first and last time,
    and for the first and last time disappear.

    You dive into vases, go rigid in objects,
    are stifled in blankets, scamper into the mirror.
    Beyond the window there are people living,
    but you don't hear their laughter
    or their weeping – you dream you don't exist.

– Is this Philip?
– Yes, this is Philip. No, this is not Philip.

    His eyes are blue, his life's a mystery,
    a frightful scar shines red above his neck.
    You don't know who this man is, he doesn't know
    himself
    if he's not part of you, or you a part of him,
            if you are not one person.

– Is this poetry?
– Yes, this is poetry. No, this is not poetry.

    There are as many truths as there are hearts.
    What's left is a sudden home, and love,
    a puff of wind.

WHAT I THOUGHT

Philippe Jaccottet
translated by Martin Sorrell

What I thought I read in him, when I dared read,
was more than surprise; astonishment really,
as though facing a dark century ahead,
sadness before this sea-surge of suffering!
What is unspeakable smashes his life's barriers.
An enveloping abyss. For defence
sadness gapes like the abyss.

Who had always loved his orchard, his walls,
the keeper of his house's keys.

ANNOUNCEMENT

Clara Janés
translated by Louis Bourne

I carry a shred of suffering
That I snatched from the look
Of an old woman,
Scraps of sorrow
I found in the satchels
Of children
Among the problems
In short division.
I collect laments,
The grief of women
Withering helplessly in the sun
On balconies,
The sadness of shy, lonely men
Who huddle
Next to heaters
Or suicide their eyes
In glasses of wine.
I look for trampled hearts,
Defeated smiles,
Thoughts of panic or weariness.

However, I must tell you
I still don't know for sure
What exactly I'll be able to do
With it all.

THE TRACK INSPECTOR'S STORY

Martti Joenpolvi
translated by Herbert Lomas

1

THE track inspector lingered on the platform as the train passed out of sight round the south bend. The previous night's shallow fall of snow retained the trail of his wife's prints, left as she went to board the train.

The porter, wearing his winter clothes already, was trundling some empty trolleys along; he nodded hello, and slowed down in case the inspector might want to have a word. But no: hardly a glance.

Didn't say much these days, the inspector.

It was a smallish station, far removed from the conurbations: a couple of sidings, one for a warehouse. Time was, a mass of freight had passed through here – you could see that from the battering of the loading platform. When the inspector first came, the traffic had flowed. Not now: one porter was more than adequate. Pulpwood – that freight had dried up years ago: the pungent smell of bark had completely vanished from the air.

A dying station it was, and the inspector knew it. That bit of rusty closed track, grassed over in the summer, those two old snowploughs nestling on it – obsolete stuff, never once used all his years in this place. Ten years now, God help us.

He came out of his trance in the waiting room, hardly knowing how he'd got there; the dusting of snow was melting off his boots. Those old wooden benches, polished with passengers' bottoms – who sat there these days? The ads for banks or tractors, they only made it more obvious that everything had come to a standstill: they intensified that feeling of total stoppage.

He was hit by giddiness: often was recently. And with it went that

46

frightening, creepy, incomprehensible sensation of unfamiliarity. Everything *should* be thoroughly familiar: the floor, with its well-worn paths of passengers' feet, the especially worn bit at the ticket office, the brasswork on the entrance door, the waiting-room smell of ingrained dirt, hot stove and piled birchwood. But it all had an air of not-there, as if it were fading away, becoming non-existent: the benches only seemed to be benches – touch them, and your hand might meet nothing solid.

Where was it coming from, this giddiness, this sudden weakness at the knees? Had even the floor been somehow consumed – eaten away by this creepy maggot of unfamiliarity?

The station master, who had been studying him from his office for quite a while, tapped on the ticket office glass with his pen. The inspector went in.

He sat for a while without a word before he said: 'Going to amalgamate, they are – linking up our section with the main line.'

The station master went tense; he glanced down at his desk, then at the inspector, then back at the items on his desk. In the silence, the ratchetty ticking of the old wall clock seemed to be getting louder. The inspector sat staring at it. The pendulum's swing, back and forth, back and forth, was as one-track as his own thoughts these days.

'You can't bloody well mean . . .'

The station master lived, with his family, in rather cramped quarters at the end of the station buildings. It was not lost on him that the news meant a move for the inspector.

'As for the wife, up to now I haven't said a word of this to her,' the inspector said, getting to his feet. 'And you as well, you know nothing about it yourself as yet. Understand?'

The station master shook his head, thinking. The inspector left the office, and the station master checked an impulse to rush off and tell his wife. At last it was coming true: his family would get the inspector's house for themselves; the porter would move into theirs.

The official residence was entirely at the inspector's disposal. Originally log-built in the early fifties, it had been weather-boarded later, and later still painted yellow. It abutted on to the station; a single-track line skirted it, but an embankment intervened, planted with several handsome birches. The previous summer the inspector had hung birdboxes on them. There was a view out on to the station yard, and in the summer the smell of sun-warmed track-ballast drifted into the rooms: the inspector loved it.

The garden, too, flaunted a few old and still-sturdy birches. There were no inside conveniences, though; and no basic improvements had ever got under way, in spite of the inspector's hopes. No doubt the authority speculated that this site would soon be redundant. As a matter of fact, the inspector's applications had not been prompted by a simple desire for an indoor tap and lavatory: he'd calculated that if the brass invested enough money in the house, they'd be less willing to close down – the thing he most dreaded. The last few days had made him realise the naivety of his dreams.

The rooms were both spacious and lofty – for some reason the government had always been keen on constructing towering rooms. There were stoves that warmed things nicely. In the autumn the authority delivered wood, ready-split, to the very door. The well was full of good clear water and, even in the hottest summers, showed no signs of drying up.

The inspector sat in his office, poring over his time-sheets. All Saints' Day glossed the figures with a snowy November light. His eyes dimmed. The pencil scrawls looked like platelayers toiling far off on some wintry straight. And what was it that was pressing on his temples and round his eyes? Were his glasses getting too weak? He shoved the time-sheets into a desk drawer: time for those tomorrow. Perhaps tonight he'd manage to get some proper sleep.

So, from the beginning of January then . . .

He'd never forget last Wednesday morning – would relive for ever the moment of the District Manager's communication, which hung before his eyes frozen, like a poster, a waiting-room ad: a tractor arrested in its mid-field ploughing, where it never snows, where starlings never flutter into the fresh furrows, an eternal autumn landscape, snowless, fallow, summer gone, winter not yet here.

The manager had tried to contact him on Tuesday in fact, but it had been Wednesday morning. After that phone call the inspector felt he couldn't ever go back to the line or meet his men again. In a single moment he'd lived through the whole space from this end-of-October Wednesday to that future first of January: now he had to slog along by main force through a time that he'd already lived through, that didn't exist.

His fingernails clutched the marbled desk pad. Hadn't he been buggered about enough? Hadn't he been through enough, at his age, practically due for pension? Servicing a backwoods railway line and bringing up a family in the sticks? Listening to all that suffocating silence piling up on him for years and years – weighing him down like snow on a fir tree? With nothing but vague carrots held out – possible vacancies in the south?

All those early years as a ganger! – living in an old shack by the railway line, originally a platelayer's hut: eaves fringed with old-fashioned white fretwork, a cowshed, an outhouse, a red-tiled cellar. July, he'd scythe the hay from the steep embankment to feed the cow, carting it home bit by bit on a trolley. Sometimes sparks from passing trains would set the haycocks burning. He'd saw up old replaced sleepers and split them for the winter fires. 1947, 1948, 1949 ... then, at last, in the mid-fifties, he was appointed track inspector, Permanent-Way Inspector. But then... what? Stuck up in the north. And so – application after written application. Till, finally, the notification that he'd been appointed to this section of line – and the understanding that he could work here until he reached pensionable age.

As the years go by, he settles down with this. Even when he begins to hear rumours of sections amalgamating, his confidence isn't too badly shaken.

Then one day a rather quiet section is to be extended; as a result a hitherto independent section will be amalgamated with a larger section and will be the responsibility of the Chief Permanent-way Inspector. In consequence the Intermediate Permanent-Way Inspector will be redundant.

That's himself.

2

There was a fire blazing in the tall office-stove. The inspector was studying his hands, reddened in the glow. Muffled music thudded from upstairs – the girls playing their records. He recognised the beat and remembered the words:

Soup plates
soup plates of blood
in Guatemala
always always

soup plates
soup plates of blood
in Guatemala
always always

He moved to his desk and spread out his time-sheets.

A long goods-train lumbered by. Trains hardly ever came this way, passenger trains scarcely at all, expresses never. Just a couple of pay-trains daily, and some of these had been laid off. The line went nowhere important; there was nothing of interest en route, not many houses even; just forest, bog, juniper-riddled bumpy ground, some rusty railway cuttings – their rock sides splitting and crumbling as the water in them froze and unfroze with the seasons. A goods-line, a metal-ore line, a backwoods-line. Outmoded track-laying. Every summer the red rosebay willowherb pushed higher and higher up the embankments; lower down, the osier, egged-on by bog, colonised more and more areas. Nobody gave a damn whether they were rooted out or not.

The inspector knew every detail of his section, miles and miles of it, every bend, every straight, every incline, the nasty bits that had to be watched, especially in heat or frost.

About mid-day the snow started again. He took a look through the kitchen window at the huge flakes wavering downwards – a shower of silence. The snow ploughs on the disused track were silhouetted white against the forest – elongated, with angular heads.

'Those coffins!' he said in mid-meal. 'Must get rid of those coffins out there. Must put in an order…'

The twins exchanged looks, puzzled, rather scared. At seventeen they were still remarkably alike. Up to now, they'd spent all their lives together. The inspector and his wife, like most parents of identical twins, had a mass of stories about their telepathic rapport. The girls had no qualms nattering about it, but when they noticed dad didn't want to know, they confined their stories to their mother. When dad was hospitalised a year ago, for his 'nerves', the girls clammed up completely about what was for them just routine stuff. More recently, the inspector had taken to looking askance at his daughters: they gave him a peculiar feeling, as if he were splitting in two.

All of a sudden he went rigid – staring at his plate. A red fluid was spreading between the islands of stew. It was blood-red. Beetroot-juice…

He sprang to his feet in the middle of the meal and shut himself in his office.

It was much later in the afternoon when he started moving again. He went upstairs to his daughters' room. He was carrying a sheepskin he used for cushioning his chair, partly because of his arthritis. Now he spread it out on the bed, inner side up:

'Ugh!' he said, recoiling from it in loathing. 'It's crawling with maggots! Little white maggots…'

The November evening was drawing in; the daylight was weak, and it was already time to light the lamp on the ceiling. The girls looked closely at the sheepskin. There was nothing odd about it.

Though they kept assuring him it was all right, he didn't seem to hear. Nor, after this, did he give the sheepskin a moment's attention. Instead he went on sitting in the cane chair till he was struck by something else: the posters on the wall were full of sneering faces. Getting up to go, he turned back again to mutter:

'Ah… what I came to say was… I'll be heating up the sauna.'

They heard the plod of their dad's heavy unsteady footsteps on the stairs. Then the outside door went bang. They ran downstairs and peeped at what he was doing through their parents' bedroom-window; the white net curtains stirred in their breath.

The virgin unbroken snow in the yard was indented with their father's fresh footprints. He was toting an armful of wood from the black doorway of the shed and heading for the sauna. Soon there was a curl of smoke from the chimney. The inspector appeared again with a snow shovel and began shifting the snow.

3

'Girls, has it ever occurred to you what things horses have to put up with?'

They were having tea.

'In the olden days they used to fight on horseback. Stuck pikes in the horses' bellies. Swords too. Right through the neck. Then when guns came, it was even worse for the horses: bullets in their guts. Your dad's seen what a horse looks like when it's dead. Swells up, I'll tell you: no shape left at all. Head and neck – that's all there is to show it was a horse.'

It was six o'clock in the evening, dark outside. But there were lights on in all the rooms: the inspector had gone rambling all over the house, lighting them. As they set the table for tea, the twins had been shaken by his rambling around: it reminded them of those other times.

After he was fifty, dad had disappeared twice – both times while they were living here. The last was two autumns ago. Mother had got on to it quickly: she'd recognised he was behaving like he'd done the first time. Some days he'd be terribly busy, talking away much more than usual. Then, other days, he'd not say a single word: just sit for hours in his office at his desk; but if the phone rang, he'd ask mother to take it – tell her to say he was off out somewhere. In the evenings he might watch the television for a while, but very soon he'd be off, rambling round from room to room. He'd go to bed for an early night but then not sleep.

Mother knew it wasn't his job that was bothering him, but pretty soon he was on the carpet for neglect. In the end the issue was settled by giving him a couple of weeks' sick leave.

At the start of the sick leave, mother kept a sharp eye on him; but he put up such a clever show, she stopped worrying. The paint was peeling on the kitchen ceiling. Dad said he'd paint it, since he had time on his hands. Everything was got together. He even put newspaper down on the floor. Work was supposed to get going the next morning, but sometime in the early hours, dad got dressed, in the office, and by morning he was nowhere to be found. Days went by. Gossip started at the station.

The second week, a postcard arrived. It was from Stockholm. You could recognise the handwriting on the address, but there wasn't a word to the family.

The two weeks' sick leave was up already, and mother had to inform the bosses about what had happened.

Then one morning something had been going on in the sauna. The floor was wet. There was damp soap on the sill. And on the floor under the bench in the changing room there was a bundle of dirty underclothes.

Two days later dad was back home. He set to work at once – and it was as if nothing had happened. Later, scraps of information came in about his travels. He'd been going round his relatives when he wasn't mooching aimlessly from one hotel or boarding house to another. One person had got a muddled letter postmarked in the north and sent registered: 'In the event of anything happening to me...' – the rest was incomprehensible. At another house he'd turned up with a bottle of brandy – but didn't drink any himself. His explanations when he did give them were unconvincing: he was on his annual vacation, or he was travelling for the government, or the long absence had made him qualify for a disability pension. Only in one place had he borrowed money.

At home they never mentioned these jaunts when dad was around, and he himself seemed to have forgotten them. The doctor told their mother there was nothing to do: her husband had committed no crime. You couldn't have someone committed because they were spreading fantasies credible enough to delude the patient. Later dad did go into hospital for a week's treatment as a voluntary patient. After that everything had gone on normally.

'Horses – they had to haul cannons, and great baggage trains: sometimes they were knee-deep on muddy roads, sometimes no roads at all. Let them get bogged down and unable to move, and they'd be flogged! Or the soldiers'd put a bullet through their heads. Good place now, though, the world: that sort of thing isn't allowed with animals any more. You'll find no statue to a horse anywhere, though. There are no eternal bonfires kept burning to commemorate the sufferings of horses! Nothing, nothing at all – unless you find an occasional memorial slab on someone or other's conscience.'

The inspector hardly ever smoked, but now he lit a cigarette. The acrid smell of stale tobacco started to envelop the room.

'Nowadays they cast sleepers out of concrete – and build embankments with gravel: you could say there's something eternal about those. Better get ready for the sauna, it's time. Off you go.'

The inspector was hunched forwards, his arms dangling between his thighs.

'Dad, shouldn't you go to bed, to rest? Forget those horses! You shouldn't be dwelling on horses all the time.'

'Horses…? It's not horses, it's snow I'm thinking about. If it keeps on coming down like this, I'll have to get those damned ploughs going for it in the morning.'

4

'You oughtn't to be off, you know,' the inspector had said to his wife the previous evening. But she could see no reason for calling off her trip, and he'd said nothing to show why he was changing his mind. It had been all right the week before when they'd talked it over.

'You really oughtn't to be off,' he'd reiterated after she'd already dropped off to sleep.

He'd turned back the quilt and looked carefully at his wife's body. It looked unfamiliar. Her shoulders had got scraggy, and her arms. Sex between them had dwindled away.

The house at night was completely silent. Their bedside lamp threw a glow on the picture on the wall opposite. The inspector gave it a long look. It had been a presentation, years ago, from his men. The twins had been two years old. The picture showed a burly angel giving two children safe conduct across a railway track. Steaming up in the background was the looming outline of a huge railway engine.

According to the men, the recipient had seen it as symbolic.

Early in the morning one of the twins spotted some odd tracks in the snow. She called her sister over to have a look. The tracks circled the outhouses and stopped by the sauna window: further than that they didn't go. It was exactly as if the person had been lifted bodily up out of his tracks.

Over breakfast the girls told their dad what they'd seen.

'Hmmm…' was all he said, slowly.

He didn't go and look. He'd got nothing on his chest but a string vest. He hadn't got his glasses with him – you could see the bridge-mark on his nose. The window sill was cushioned with a light white coating of snow. The forest – yesterday it had been a dark belt encircling the view – had been blanched completely overnight. The snowploughs on the disused track were almost invisible against it.

The inspector said he was off to the attic to get his felt snowboots out.

'Snowboots! On a Sunday!'

'Yes, the time's come,' he said.

They could hear their dad stumping up stairs to the top floor, opening the attic door. There was a narrow garret running along the whole of one side of the house. It was crammed with cardboard boxes and various bits of obsolete gear. Distinct dusty beams and a dim light filtered through narrow windows.

The girls could hear the muffled sounds of their father thudding about up there; then there was a heavier thump, as if a great weight had been shifted.

Ten minutes later, since there was still no sound of dad coming back – in fact no sound at all – Anita decided she'd go up and look.

Almost at once there was her shrill cry, and then another, more smothered.

Anja ran up to the attic.

Then she saw too.

SNOW IN SUNSHINE

Ole Korneliussen
translated by Anne Born

S O that's how you can spend Saturday night. I've been with my mates since yesterday afternoon. It was a great night, we were on the beer as usual. But not a lot, we're all pretty skint just now. In fact we had so little it was only just enough to make us thirsty. That was OK though, for tonight I've decided to keep my head clear. You shouldn't spend such an important evening half legless. Even if we didn't drink much, the mood was good, and when the pub closed and we went our separate ways, we shouted goodnight to each other and fixed a time when we'd meet again. It was a really great evening, and now and again I completely forgot how it was going to end. Not till I'd left the lads and was on my own did I realise I'd lied to them. Because I'd decided that I would never see these people again. Not them, not anyone. Because I'd been enjoying myself with happy people I'd been happy with them, but I'd acted as if I was happier that I really was. Probably a good thing, that, for if my mates had known what I had in mind the evening would certainly have taken on another colour.

When I was on my own, as I didn't want to meet anyone, I went up to the top of the rocks where no one ever goes at this time of day. I sat down at the top and looked out over the town. It's something I often do on a summer evening when dusk is falling, just sit looking out over the town. I've seen all this since my childhood. When there's light in the eastern sky on summer nights the town is in half darkness, the street lights come on, it's as if it changes character and gets more unreal, as if all that's revealed so mercilessly by daylight disappears. It makes the town seem friendlier. Perhaps inside myself I'm afraid of the daylight, since I'd rather look out over the town when dusk is falling, when the contours are wiped out and everything takes on a touch of unreality.

Wonder who'll be sitting here tomorrow at this time? It won't be me anyway. Wonder where I'll be? I'll have turned into nothing, I guess. And I couldn't care a toss about that.

Look, there's smoke coming up from the chimney down there, wonder why they're lighting the stove so late at night? It isn't all that cold. Probably they're going to cook something, a lot of them have something to eat before going to bed, especially if they've had a jar or two during the evening. The house down there is one of the few that still use coal in the old-fangled manner. There's not a breath of wind, so the smoke goes straight up, higher and higher until you can't see it any more. That's what life's like too. To start with it's clear but soon you can't make it out. I'm alive as long as I breathe, but what life is really all about remains a puzzle. It doesn't matter anyway that I don't understand it, because if I did I'm sure I'd find it completely pointless.   /

When you sit up here and study the town you get an idea of what goes on in life. By looking at the way the houses and the other buildings are arranged down there, you see how it all connects up. The churchyard has been in use many years and it's almost full up now. For the first fifty years it was only half full but the rest have come just in the last fifteen. There certainly have been a lot of deaths in recent years. And then people do say that in the old days people died of relatively mild illnesses. But now that we have a hospital, more and more die. The hospital has been enlarged several times, the numbers of doctors and other staff increased, but still more and more people die. No matter how clever the medics are, no matter how good their facilities, they can't give us eternal life, though they can probably make life a bit pleasanter for us. Ha – it's a good thing the hospital isn't ten times bigger still, or there probably wouldn't be a soul left alive in town.

The whole of life is centred on the churchyard. Anyone looking down on the town from up here can see that. The churchyard is in the centre, then beyond it there's the crèche and the nursery school, then the school and the youth club. And nearest the churchyard is the old people's home. When you leave school you can live either in one of the houses or apartment blocks until you go to the old people's home, and once you move in there there's only one place left. A little way away is the hospital, which funnily enough has the car repair workshop and the fire station for neighbours. If your outboard motor breaks down you can get it repaired at the car workshop just next to the hospital. If you break your leg you can get it mended at the hospital just next to the car repair shop. If the outboard is totally burned out you can chuck it on the tip, and when you die you're stuffed into the churchyard. It's surprising really that the tip and the churchyard are so far apart.

I've heard it said that when they decided the town needed to be enlarged, each summer a whole crowd of Danes came to measure up the land so they could see where the houses and other buildings should be built. When they were messing around down in Copenhagen in the winter getting bored with drawing maps, I'm quite sure they arranged the buildings like this to make fun of us. Or they showed us without realising it what a lifespan looks like. From the crèche the road leads straight via the school and the old people's home to the churchyard. In between you can get the necessary repairs done at the hospital or the car repair shop. Such is life.

Well, perhaps it's good enough as it is. Anyway, I can't change it. You can ask as many questions as you like, you'll never get a proper answer. Everyone has his own explanation, after all. But one thing is certain: we are alone when we come out of our mother, and we are also alone when we die. These are my thoughts now, like the starving man who thinks of nothing but food.

What are we really born for? When I was younger I never had these thoughts, my life went along with the seasons. In the autumn I looked forward to Christmas and when that was over I looked forward to the coming of spring with lots of sunshine, and when the snow started to melt I looked forward to the summer and school holidays. Only when you have something to look forward to can you enjoy life, a lot even. Before I went to school I looked forward to starting and admired people who were already there. I remember clearly how proud I was if I managed to punch one of them. While I was at school I looked forward like mad to finishing, because when you left school you were thought of as a grownup and could behave like a grownup.

In our last year of school there was a lot of discussion about what job or what training we'd start on afterwards. My parents stressed how important it was for me to get regular and secure work. When you're an adult and have a fixed job, what's the next thing you can look forward to?

I don't think there's anything for me to look forward to. It's several weeks now since I finished school, I'm on summer holiday, and I've no idea what to do afterwards. There's nothing I feel like doing. I'm always tired now, and nothing at all grabs me. When I was at school my parents and teachers decided everything for me. They told me what to do and for the most part I let them decide. If I just did what they said, they let me go round suiting myself. Several times I've tried doing things in my own way, but every single time I found it only led to trouble. It's very hard for people to let you do things in your own way. Only if you go along with others' wishes and norms do they think you're a nice guy. But if you allow yourself to do things in your own way they're all down on you like a shot. It seems that if you want to be something, you have to go along with others' wishes and do exactly what everyone else does. You mustn't have ideas of your own but do all you can to conform to general opinion. If you want a pleasant and well-paid job you'd better join the party currently in power. Do as the dogs do. Agree with the strongest. And if you think differently, don't let it be noticed. No, I say, shit, they're not getting me to live like that.

They say you get stronger if you help carry the common burden. I've never understood why that strength is so important. You don't notice you've got it until you make use of it. It's like having money in your pocket and not spending it. You don't notice you've got it until you spend it. Picture a crowd of people carrying a big crate. Most of them make the effort without saying anything, but then suddenly one of them shouts: 'Togetherness is strength! Use your muscle!' Well, if he's got so much to spare that he can shoot his big mouth off, something tells you he's not putting enough into it but only wants one thing, and that's to lord it over the ones who are really straining themselves. There's only one thing to be said to someone like that: 'Shut your mouth and get on with it!'

I decided long ago I wouldn't join in carrying that crate. I would do what I wanted, no one was going to decide for me. If you share the load you can also reckon on others helping you when you're in a tough spot. That's how it is in the animal world, at least. If you want to survive you must stay with the herd. If you leave it you can be sure of being attacked and wiped out by other animals. That's how Nature arranged it. Now I have decided that before this night is out I shall show myself and the others that I will not take part in carrying the load and so I will annihilate myself. I won't be like the other poor berks. Because if, just for the sake of peace, you let other people push you around and overrule you, you'll never be able to do anything yourself. It's true some of them say they've thought of breaking out, but they daren't do it, because they're scared of being different. I feel really sorry for them. But I am not scared, and before it gets light early tomorrow, I'll show them I dare. Of course they'll say I ran away from it all because I didn't dare go along with them, but I don't give a shit what they say. I know in myself I'm doing it because I dare to.

It's getting really dark now so I shall go over to the place where it's going to happen. There's no point going on sitting here when you can't see anything properly. It's dark, but as it's high summer the sky is already getting pale in the east, and in a couple of hours it will be quite light and the sun will rise. It looks as if it'll be a fine day. Pity I didn't see the sunset, I was in the pub with the lads then. I'd have liked to see the sunset, for I'll never see it again now.

The light is coming. Incidentally, it's always surprised me that so much is said and written about dawn and twilight in our country.

In the first light of morning/Carlsberg's flowing all over the sea/Tuborg's flowing all over the sea/It was my brother/ my last brother/he was assaulted by snaps/a big bottle of snaps/and sank./I wish the earth would split.

That's a very nice tune, we often sang it at school, but it makes me think of my cousin's funeral. Because my cousin, who was three years older than me, died last summer. I was very fond of him. He was a very happy person with great faith in the future. He was only just over eighteen when he bought himself a new 16-foot boat. He was so pleased with it he bought a 40 horse power outboard motor for it. His father told him off for putting such a pow-erful motor on such a light little boat, but he replied that it would save time getting him out to the fishing grounds and back. His father had accepted that. And that summer my cousing did very well with his fishing.

One day when he hadn't been catching a lot, he was on his way home and passed some of his friends just as they emptying their net. As their cutter was fully loaded they told my cousin he could fill up his boat with the cod they didn't have room for. He wasn't going to say no to that so he filled the boat right up the gunwhale.

While he was quite slowly making for home with his heavy cargo he was surprised by a sudden storm in the middle of the fjord. To save the over-loaded boat from sinking he had to throw a lot of cod overboard. He was in the gravest danger and only just managed to get back. I was down on the quay when he arrived and I remember he was wet through even though he had the best rainwear money can buy, he was shaking all over and deathly pale. His rifle was wet through too. I inherited that rifle, and it's real good. He sold the cod that was left that afternoon, and made good money. When the pub opened he went in with his pals to live it up a bit. He said money that had cost him so much trouble but all the same had been easily earned, ought to be used to enjoy yourself with. That night my cousin spent all the money on beer and snaps and got very drunk. He didn't go home before the pub closed but instead of going to bed he went out again in his boat early next morning. He told his girlfriend he wanted to go out to join the people he'd met the day before at the good fishing place, and he took his father's full tank of petrol and went off.

They think he must have fallen asleep while he raced out at full speed and hit an ice floe. The first fishermen to go out in the morning found his boat adrift with the bow ripped right open, and they were convinced he had been thrown overboard with the collision. His body was not found for several days. It was very sad.

His father reacted rather strangely, maybe from shock and sorrow. For some days after the accident no one heard him talk of anything but the fine full tank of petrol his son had taken out with him. But he soon came to himself again. Yes, it was that tune I was thinking of. It was when my cousin was buried. The church service was finished and we'd got to the churchyard and were about to lower his coffin into the grave when his girlfriend started to cry and sing that tune. The melody is well known but she had written the words herself.

In the first light of morning/Carlsberg flows all over the sea/Tuborg flows all over the sea/it was my brother/ my eldest brother/he was hit by snaps/a big bottle of snaps/and sank./I wish the earth would crack.

And she went on crying and screaming and nothing the others could do would calm her. She grew more and more confused, and before night they took her to the hospital. As her condition didn't change in the following days she was flown by helicopter to the hospital at Godthåb, and she only recovered enough to go home just before Christmas. After that it wasn't long before she found a new boyfriend, and now she's pregnant. Yesterday I saw her waddling along like Donald Duck with a big stomach. Each time I meet her she assures me that no matter how much they try to make her, she won't let her child be called after my cousin. Why should it be so important to call babies after dead people? But I'm sure she'll give the child an old

Greenlandic name. It's become quite the fashion now. Most children are given old Greenlandic names because folk love to ape each other. When one starts, the rest of the flock follow with their aping.

When they brought my cousin's boat home I saw that the only one of his things that hadn't sunk was his rifle. He usually tied it tightly to the thwarts. His father gave it to me and said he knew I'd be glad to have it. It's a really good rifle, so when I'd given it a thorough clean and rubbed oil into it, it was as good as new. I shot many animals with it through the winter, and it's really good for shooting-matches too. A first-class rifle that works every time. Now it's all ready and well hidden in the place where I'm going. Before it's light I shall use it for the last time. I wonder who will inherit it from me? Perhaps it will just be thrown away, but that would be a shame for such a good rifle. When I use it for the last time I shall only fire once and that can't hurt it at all. OK, I don't care, let them throw it away, if that's what they want. I'll be thrown away too. Since my cousin was buried last summer, they've already buried about ten people. Three old ones, a baby that had been sickly from birth, the rest young people under twenty.

Look, there's a car moving along down there. What the hell's it doing here at night? Even the police don't go out much now. There's not much for them to do these days. This summer isn't at all like last summer. It's as if it doesn't really want to come, it's still cold and the warm weather seems to be waiting even though it's the middle of July. There are no fish either and people have hardly any money to speak of. Only those who work on land can earn something, for the fishermen these are hard times. That's why it's so quiet in the town even on Saturday nights. The old people say it's nice and peaceful but the youngsters think it's dead boring. Now and then the police drive round a bit. They're bored too.

I recognise the car that's going along down there now, it's one of GTO's cars. Almost everyone employed by the government has a car at their disposal for work, but they use it for a lot of things besides the job. Even after knocking-off time you can see all these cars driving around the town. That one must be on his way down to see to his boat, and as the weather is good, that's quite unnecessary. He has a good big boat down in the harbour, he only uses it to go out for trips in his free time. That's probably why my parents so badly want me to get a good fixed job, because only those with good fixed jobs on land can afford to have a good big boat and a free car at their disposal. That may well be something to covet, but what the hell's the good of having a boat if you can't use it when you feel like it because you have to be at work. It must be frustrating to have a good big boat lying there if you can't go out when the weather's fine. No, you must wait patiently till knocking-off time or the weekend. Such is life. The fishermen can't afford good big boats, but those who work ashore can afford them but can't really use them.

I often see old people, many of them with bad legs, toiling along with their modest shopping bags, while public employees, as a rule people in their prime, can't move a couple of meters without hopping into a car. And then they say the public employees are public servants. It's well known that most of them who are well up the ladder only think of themselves. Shits. That one down there has stopped just above the place where his boat is safely moored. He won't even get out of his car, just turn it round and drive back. I wonder who pays for his petrol?

He makes me mad. Now it's quite dark, I think I'll go down there and smash up his car before going on to where I've decided. I've heard that if you put sugar in the petrol tank it ruins the engine. The carburettor and cylinders will burn right out. I could puncture his tyres with a knife too, of course. But he won't discover that till tomorrow if the weather's fine and he wants to go down to his boat for a trip. No, what the hell, I can't be fagged. What's it matter when I won't be able to be there to see how bloody daft he'll look when he can't get his car to go? Pity I didn't get the idea earlier or I'd have done it. Now it's pointless. Everything's pointless. I'm just sitting here doing nothing, starting to get cold even though it's summertime. The sky in the east is getting lighter and lighter, so I'd better get going to the place.

The place where it's to be, I chose it long ago. It's just right for the purpose. Our town is actually divided in two. Over to the west is the old town where people lived before there were so many and there weren't yet any plans for extension. The big buildings from colonial times are still there. They are protected and well maintained and let out to Danish work people. In colonial times the Danish rulers worked in these buildings, now it's the new masters, the independent Danish tradespeople who have moved in, and like their predecessors they employ many Greenlanders. Around these buildings were the Greenlanders' little turf houses, but they have all been removed. No doubt they found them too sordid and were ashamed of them. I've never seen a house like that, never seen how my forefathers lived. But I can see the houses my forefathers' masters built.

Some way away from the old town lies the new one, built in the fifties. I was born and grew up in that part of the town and have only thought of the old town as a place you went to look around as a spectator. The new town has everything: shops, schools, hospital, electricity plant and many apartment blocks, yes, everything. And between these two completely different towns there is an area of rocks and stones, that is protected as well. When the new building was under way in the fifties and sixties, that was not touched. It's a great place to be in among all the rock formations and stones, and when you sit there you get a feeling of being far far away. No wonder it's a favourite place for excursions when the weather's fine. When the afternoon sun really warms you can see people walking there with their carrier bags and cardboard boxes and with expectant smiles on their faces. That's why there are so many empty beer cans and bottles amongst the rocks.

Last night when I couldn't sleep I got up and dressed. Then I packed the rifle, which I inherited from my cousin, into a black plastic bag and carried it out there and hid it among the stones. It's so well hidden you have to know where it is to find it. I knew already then why and how it would be used. I'd made my decision. Now I am going to carry it out without being disturbed by anyone. The rocky area is far enough away from the nearest house to prevent any of the sleepers hearing a rifle shot. And if anyone did hear it they would not think anything of it, there are plenty of noises in the night.

Before I start down from my rocky lookout post I'll just make sure that the two cartridges I put into my pocket with my cigarettes are safely there. Yes, they are. Ah well, no point in hanging about, better get it over with quickly. I'll jog, even though my legs are stiff from sitting so long, and now I can feel how good it is to be on the point of getting something done that you've decided on and want to do. Jogging along I soon reach the place where I hid the rifle. That's good, no one has found it. I'm not afraid. What is there to be afraid of? I know I won't feel anything. When I'm taking the rifle out of the plastic bag I discover my hands are wet with sweat, even though the night is cool. I'll find myself a really good place to sit. Oh no, there've been people here today and they've chucked their beer cans everywhere, so there's no choice but to settle down among empty beer cans and get out a cartridge. Well, I must be a bit nervous after all, I've dropped it. Lucky I've got a spare one. I push it into the breech and then aim the barrel of this wonderfully good rifle, that works every time, at my head.

Just as the sun rises in the east a rifle shot rings out to the west of the town. Not one person hears it.

The morning brings the loveliest sunny weather. The most eager ones are out early, some sail westwards, others go deeper into the fjord, happy that summer has come. Some, though, are still asleep, and others are getting up with heavy heads and dry mouths. Some wake up to realise they have not slept in their own beds but have overstepped the sixth commandment in the nicest possible manner, though they in no way feel sinful. Others again sit over their morning coffee quietly and peacefully, they have decided to have a really lazy day. And quite a few are getting ready to go to church.

At about half past nine there's a brief shower of sleet. No one takes much notice of it. It's high summer, nothing to worry about. But those who look up at the sky see the little black cloud that brought snow with it drifting by. Still, that doesn't make anyone out of all these people enjoying their Sunday recall the old saying from our forefathers' day, that if you see a snowcloud while the sun is shining it's a sign that a human being has taken his own life.

SWEDEN

Kristoffer Leandoer
translated by Anne Born

The January day hides from us
wrapped in its pale mist.
The sun's diluted all over the sky,
the light that falls has only spilled out
and can hardly cut shadows for us.
We travel through Sweden unopposed.
The horizon line backs off by mutual agreement.

Along the E4 the land's going grey
into Saturday afternoon.
The fields slowly peter out
of their own contours.
In every courtyard the mystery
of laid-aside tools thickens
while lamps are lit inside.

The birchbole keeps playing
the same endless game of blind chess
where not a single man may move.
There's no possible reconciliation
between black and white,
between guest and reality,
background and contour.

Outside Södertalje they're playing football
on a fenced gravel ground
in the sleet's flickering image.
They jump and slither up and down
without ever scoring a goal
while darkness thickens over the ground
till not a single one can be seen.

And it's not true
that we've never taken sides.
We've just stayed outside.

MY IMAGINATION IS PARTICULAR

Bronisław Maj
translated by Adam Czerniawski

My imagination is particular: it sees
a tear, a curious leaf in the shivering feathery plume
of a maple, a line on a face I came to love
fresh and young. It's also banal:
prepared to accept as the essence of things
what I am observing now: on a secluded path
the casual encounter of a boy
with a squirrel, which is cautiously approaching
his beseechingly outstretched hand,
moved by hunger, unconscious of the light
which – now kindled – will not die
in the grown-up man. My imagination
doesn't even need the bounds of the possible:
it's not terrified by the yellow (or violet)
flash, which will burn the sun, by a gust
of sticky dust, by the thrust of pain
beneath the skull, which will end everything.
It sees it as nothing. Nothing instead
of the face that I love. Of the maple. Nothing
instead of the essence of things fulfilling itself
in a communion between beast and man.
Nothing of the essence of things. Nothing –
beyond imagination.

YOUR HANDS

Joyce Mansour
translated by Martin Sorrell

Your hands' blind machinations
On my trembling breasts
Slow motion of your paralysed tongue
In the pathos of my ears
All my beauty drowned in your stone eyes
Death in your stomach feeding on my brains
All this makes me a strange lady

SEASIDE SILENCE

Adriaan Morriën
translated by Ria Leigh-Loohuizen

I WAS born before the First World War in Yjmuiden. My father was a sail-maker, my mother the daughter of a fisherman. Those circumstances alone meant that our house was cramped for space, a notion I wasn't only unaware of during my childhood, as I was of so many other notions that were not tested until later by my sensory powers, but the weight of which only started to press on me somewhat when I, too, began to long for a room of my own. That happened around the age of fourteen, after discovering one memorable night that I was able to masturbate and realised at the same time, with the faultless instinct of the youthful miscreant, that I must not do it in the livingroom and had better be silent about such a skill in front of my parents.

It would be years before my mother, when we were at home alone together and it was a convenient moment, attempted to make clear to me in guarded terms how harmful to body and soul such a habit was. We were sitting in the front room, in the second house of my childhood, on the sofa, a piece of furniture that had been introduced into our home as well as others as a status symbol of the lower class. I deemed it preferable to let the subject rest, for the sake of my mother's soul, but I was very well aware how plucky and courageous she, an unlettered, thoroughly Christian woman, had been in bringing up the subject, and also how much it was a token of her care, her affection for me. I was astonished to discover that she, in her circumstances, had knowledge of the phenomenon so dubious to her, but I didn't dare question her about it. Those were different times. Each object in the house was from the start a witness and, with hindsight, a confirmation thereof. Later I realised how many riddles and misunderstandings we leave behind in our parental home when we have outgrown it. I found that unbearable for a long time, but I have become reconciled to it. I would perhaps think of my parents much less often if we had understood each other completely.

Yjmuiden originated in 1876 on the mouth of the North Sea Canal, which provided Amsterdam with a less cumbrous entrance to the oceans of the world, a situation which as a boy filled me with a certain pride and through which I became familiar with the capital, or it with me, although I didn't visit it more than five or six times before I was thirty. When I was growing up in Yjmuiden it was a town that hardly had a past, an unhistoric settlement, so to say, come about by a wilful attack on nature, a watery fault in the incomparable dune area of Kennemerland. Unhistoric meant that I, or whoever, nowhere trod in the imaginary footsteps of famous men and women, citizens who were born or had lived there centuries ago and performed ingenious, heroic or sacrificing deeds. Not one house, pointed out to me by my parents during our Sunday stroll, with a tablet or a commemorating plaque. Not one illustrious grave in the cemetery. No statue anywhere. Not one allusion or glorification, cast in stone or metal, of the imaginary that still had to begin for Ijmuiden and of which I wouldn't be able to claim even now that it has taken root yet. When I started to write my first poems in the twenties, I assumed, not even mistakenly perhaps, that I was the first one who did something like that there, on that sandy, shell-ridden ground. During my haughtiest moments that were at the same time my loneliest, I felt myself a pioneer in the missing, an advocate in the thin atmosphere of the mother tongue.

No sound historic reminiscences in the town of my birth. Nor any remarkable architecture, daring or skilfull city planning in a town, born of chance and opportunity, like a child out of wedlock, intended for fishermen, craftsmen and small tradesmen. When the canal approached completion, the first predictable housing developments arose in the vicinity of the locks: simple uniform dwellings for the lock personnel. Fishing, initially practised from the beach and the embankments, expanded so fast that in no time the fishing harbour had been dug. Between the harbour and the canal, on a triangular, peninsula-like site, the oldest town centre arranged itself, gradually expanding inland during my childhood, as if the growth of my environment kept abreast of my own and that of my friends. That oldest part consisted of some stretched-out parallel streets with obvious names: Canal Street, Sea Street, Neptune Street, Prince Henry Street. The name of the quay across from the station yard, the first showpiece in town, the middle-class imitation of a boulevard where the well-to-do settled, was reserved for Queen Wilhelmina.

The names of the side streets were, I assume, given good-naturedly or from embarrassment, so that I, quite appropriately perhaps, first saw the light of day in one of the streets remembered with a simple girl's name: Anna Street. Later in my life the name Anna, in various personifications and even in my dreams, would play a role of attractive significance, as if a prediction had come true. In order to give strength to the prediction, Anna Street was crossed by Adriana Street. There was also an Emma Street and even an Emma Square, lined with trees, practically the only trees in the vicinity of my parental home, trees we could hear sigh as a relief in summer, when the wind came from the east. Yjmuiden seemed petrified right from the start, a town without gardens, shrubbery or parks, windy, quickly chilled and often a bit godforsaken, in spite of the activity, the noise of the fishermen and fortune seekers, and in spite of the churches, big and small, that shot up like mushrooms, for soon countless faiths dined at the same table in Yjmuiden.

Godforsaken; on empty scorched Sunday afternoons when no auctions were held, there was often a fearsome stink behind the fishmarket, as if a massacre, executions had taken place there. But on the other hand, one short walk and you were by the sea or in the most beautiful dune landscape, where your footsteps made partridges fly up. The view of the sea banned all timidity. The dunes in their dancing protection offered shelter to feelings I wasn't yet capable of expressing. However much I have felt misplaced, in all relativity, in my Calvinistic milieu, I didn't feel really locked up in my birth town. The sea, if only because of its closeness and its grandness as a natural phenomenon, offered an awareness of future freedom. I was not really imprisoned, the way you perhaps are, or fear to be, when you have been born more inland, in villages and landscapes that lack perspective or, when it is present at all, stabilises the irrefutability of destiny.

The ships that came sailing through the canal from all the corners of the world or that stood out to sea beyond the piers, those last embraces of the continent, robbed our parochialism of oppression. That same circumstance also prevented the origination of a village culture that connected to such a tradition in our fatherland. Yjmuiden remained a child out of wedlock that would somehow always remain a ne'er-do-well. The minds were too scattered and contradictory for a flourishing community. The atmosphere remained turbulent, the feeling hard or sentimental. Mockery was highly regarded. The war, the second one, put an end to everything. The majority of the population was evacuated in 1942. Yjmuiden, too, has known its dispersion, its diaspora. I suspect that many people from Yjmuiden didn't return to their place of birth after the war. I made my home in Amsterdam, the only city I feel at home in on a large as well as a small scale.

I have remarked that our family was cramped for space, and also that it didn't oppress me during my early childhood. Especially not, I think, since our family, against Calvinistic dogma, remained limited. My father did not fuck my mother to death, as some other church members did. When I was born I had a brother and a sister who were two and three years older than me respectively. I remained the youngest for eight years, an enviable position that offered ample opportunity for adoring my mother as the little lover of hers I was, without already having to yield my place to a younger brother after two or three years. I am convinced that that schooling in intimacy has strengthened and deepened my feeling for sensualness.

Our house consisted of a livingroom with adjacent kitchen, in which the toilet was also located. On the street side there was a small room, the best room, in which we only drank coffee adorned with a shortbread biscuit on Sundays after church. So, all things considered, we actually had a surplus of living space. In the short corridor was a staircase leading to the attic, where once, after I had been naughty, my father had locked me up and I was scared out of my wits. We washed in the kitchen, at the tap, our hands with soft soap, our faces with Sunlight soap. On Saturday evening my mother would fetch the sink tub that was secured to the wall with a nail in the small courtyard, and changed us, as it was called; first my sister, then my brother and me. We were provided with clean underclothes that had to last us for a week – underpants, shirt, vest, that we kept on when going to sleep in one of the box beds in the livingroom, the bottom one for the children and the top one for the parents, sleeping cupboards that were closed off by two doors and that were all too cosy. A beam of light from the lamp over the table penetrated through a chink. We heard our parents talking, in muted voices, so as not to prevent us from falling asleep. But however much we exerted ourselves to hear what they talked about, sleep relentlessly took possession of us with its secretive, innate power that once, in an absolute form, will be our death.

MORAL EPISTLE TO MYSELF

Blas de Otero
translated by Louis Bourne

You say 'Life,' and think, what,
When saying 'I should write,' 'I'm going,'
'I'm very sorry you don't understand'?
What do you think when saying 'I'm choking'?

For life's simple. It consists
Of smoking, living together, stirring an arm
And making others be born between a woman's
Legs: the bridge Jorge Manrique

Overlooked in that ballad
About the river. What are you thinking?
Life's beautiful from the film's
Start to when we light a smoke.

You say man passes, time flies
And Spain goes on between Atlantic
And Mediterranean, decorating its
Altamira cave in a false décor.

But don't brood so much about Old Castile,
About La Mancha's stain worn on our cheeks.
Life's no joke, the Istanbul poet
Said when jailed.

Neither is Spain. At bottom,
It's too serious. Why say 'I'm choking'
If it doesn't even rhyme, however imperfect
It is (your country)? And now, too much so.

Don't think the whole of life is this
Dead hand, this past revived.
There are other brilliant days to compensate,
And you've seen them. They gave you bearings.

All things have their end. Throw away
Those thoughts, and let's head for the country
To see the laundress's loveliness
Before the river dies in her arms.

VERONICA M.
TELLS HER NEIGHBOUR

Konstanty Puzyna
translated by Adam Czerniawski

They lay strangely tangled up.
Must have taken something as soon as
the Gestapo knocked at dawn. A pale sun
scurried along the ceiling to the ringing door.
Throat's all dried up someone grassed they're finished
and us that's it. Jesus! But no.
They came for Jurek. But Jurek's clever
not seen since Easter. *Seit Ostern? du lügst!*
But maybe they knew. Trying to panic me.

And then you know the explosion and I shelter in the
            doorway.
Arms flying the heat swirling spilled frogs
my man crouched with a fag his face sweating
then the silence and it's over. And such a hole a crater.
Everything seems normal again the carts going to market
but us we're in thick fog. You're stunned you touch
a vase the kitchen tap and that's it you don't think
about the beets for the borsch about margarine being short.
It wasn't till 7 that I knocked.

They lay tangled up in that Jewish fate.
The bed in a mess his hand on hers
and a drop of water in the mug. Evenings
after curfew the windows blacked-out
we would have them to supper. They always
asked for news and about Jurek. They loved
a good joke and told us about balls and travels
what it's like in Vienna at the opera the clothes
and now this mug. Nearly three years
they were with us.

I said to my man they went together see
you drunk. You lecher.

So we carried up two sacks of coal from downstairs.

WHAT NEVER FADES

Claudio Rodríguez
translated by Louis Bourne

To the little girl, Reyes

These children who sing
And lift up life
In the circle games of the world,
Which are not walls but open doors
Where if you once go in
You truly never leave,
For you never leave the miracle.
Here there are no locks,
Sets of nails, or ironwork,
Nor bells, not even cracks in doors,
But innocence, freedom, fate.
These children who call sky heaven
Because it's so far up,
And who have seen sleep,
Sky blue with white beauty spots,
Dance with a mouse among childhood's
Generous and awful furniture,
Mysterious too.
There in that table leg
Hope, today memory, remains;
And on the back of that armchair, a cruel,
Warm and virgin nest;
And in that wardrobe, fear's radiance
When, opening it, you never
Know if there are wasps or honey,
Clothes or their clean sky.

Claudio Rodríguez

These children who break money
As though it were eggshells
And know numbers
Don't skip rope because they have weak
Legs, except for the three,
And know how
Ash whispers in the wolf's teeth.

How many times, unworthy,
I have been beside this circle,
Beside this dome,
Beside the children who have no shadow.
And I hear it sing, alive and firm,
And it delights and accuses me,
So full of tenderness and secrets,
Offered and useless till now
In gardens, squares and streets,
Even in one's breathing,
One's pulse and essential
Caress, one's bright kiss.

I am gazing now at the littlest girl,
The one who puts her childhood
Beneath the logs.
She must be saved. She sings and dances clumsily
And must be saved.
That gentle quality in her clumsiness
Should be saved.
It gives love. She's a blonde girl
With blue eyes, so blue
They almost sadden. I never
Had that wonderful sure light.

You must be saved. Come here.

Come close, I don't know, no,
But I want to tell you
Something maybe no one's told you,
A story now for me a lament.
Come, come and feel
The rain fall pure like you,
Hear its sweet sound, and how
It gives us song for
Sorrow and injustice. Come, come on,
Blessed pollen, give me
Your brightness, your freedom,
Straighten your lemon-yellow
Ribbon. I want your hair
To stir more, I want you to raise
Your ribbon's adventure higher up
And your body to be ringing and redeeming.

I follow the circle,
Live in it, right out at sea
With these children,
Never captive but with fertile
Seed in soul while the rain is falling.

I only ask, when the years
Have passed, that I may
Go back into this pure, lasting body
With the heartbeat I have now,
Back into this circle,
This house open for ever.

DECREE ABSOLUTE

Eira Stenberg
translated by Herbert Lomas

> *If you're afraid of loneliness,*
> *don't get married.*
> Anton Chekhov

1.

A fierce wind turned us back into one,
knotted arms and legs around our body,
fastened them tightly
                        hurtfully,

and I never, never wanted to be free...

but the Norns had come:
we followed the laws of dreaming:
slowly you became a wall
and I the ivy
dumbly hanging down your stone side.

Oh cursed Norns,
weren't those ancient tragedies enough?
I'd have constructed
the plot of this play differently, if I could.

I didn't want heart's blood in my inkwell.

2.

Slowly I free your hand from my skin,
slowly the warmth fades –
I start to feel cold.
I mole my way through the years,
past the rusted guns
till I find
the sign engraved on stone.
I collect a museum round me
to cover you up.
And still your face comes back
like an image on water
after the stone is thrown.
I've thrust you aside
only to dream you.
For I can only love
hopelessly.
I'm condemned to kiss the face
I've created myself.
How sorry I am for myself...

3.

Now I'm in earnest.
I'm trying to tell about the man I
reached to uselessly,
till I finally loosed
that angry arrow to drop him –
near me at last.

Anger and longing embraced:
crazy consorts on life's way.

I want to bury that embrace deep
in the common grave of humanity's partings:
say my goodbyes in the ancient dirges,
the old women's wailings
I was never taught.

It's wretched to weep without words!
If only there were keeners still teaching
the secrets of saying goodbye.
But this is a time of breaking words and homes.
You have to study a new speech.
The ghosts of mouldered homes
Still colonise the two-room flats, the rented rooms,
the mortgaged concrete coops
until they go bang:
the three-piece suites slide slowly down the stairs
and the children, the dear children
fall into the new age without a tear.

Women were taught to seek a man
and now they seek themselves,
seek a woman, go inside themselves.

There, in the great hall of mirrors,
they meet the mothers and the grandmothers,
the giggling girls that romp with ribbons in their hair
like silk-winged butterflies.
They ask names, each others' names:
they've been so busy they've forgotten
to get to know themselves.
Like a shadow that clings,
they've doubled their husband's life,

their husband's and their children's.
Their clock has been a sundial.

But all at once among the ruined homes,
they see the moon:
pregnant-bellied, white, it watches
the removal men leaving;
they see the rise and ebb
that even the ocean-going liners must observe.
They see the moon's changing shapes,
her thin crouching back
as she bends by the stove
with the ruling dark of timelessness around her.

And the troops of shrieking girls stop:
they look quietly at the light
spilling radiant and unburning
into the shadow of the world's dreams.

I too bend towards my love,
I smooth the soiled shoulder
I so much loved,
I straighten his man's back.
Now, while he's still stunned from his fall,
I kiss his eyes
criss-crossed by the crow's feet of tiredness,
I kiss his mouth,
where silence lives
(the secret coffer of separations).

And now, right now I should be able
to lead out the ancient dirges of my grief

lest I howl like a beast
or tear the heart out of my chest –
hoping to grow a new one –
fresh as a flooding cluster of opening lilac.

Spring doesn't come like that.
The roots must thrust
deep down
where the warmth defies the changes of weather
and stays alive.
I must remember patience
and cherish the girl
who, over and over again,
goes to the rendezvous
and changes, as she approaches, into a woman.

4.

We built our nest in an old tree.
We went rejoicing into marriage.
No one invited
griefs
as guests of honour:
we'd no idea that grief must be regaled,
the past wept for,
or it comes uninvited,
at the wrong moment.

They were waiting in the branches, croaking.
We'd nested in the family tree –
a thorn hidden in the flesh
that dropped sour fruits.

A chance riffle of the leaves –
mothers, fathers, children –
and a terrible quarrel filled the room, and tears.

Still, the trunk was carved with a heart.

5.

I took what was offered:
a familiar-looking happiness.
We two, and then that third,
a tiny tot looking like you.
So simple,
till the dead raised their heads
from the sod and burst out laughing.

Fantasy the whole floor:
the past was spawning fungi.

6.

The old story: Hurry off to Paradise.
We jogged the sawdust track that
gradually hardened into gravel.
'Faster, faster,' yelled the old jackdaws
spectator-sporting in the branches.
We'd thought we were at home,
the home was ours,
till we heard their 'chak'.
The home was inhabited by the ages.

7.

Year by year the room sprouted a thicket of willows
and an idle crowd.
'Needs a clean, this place,' you said.
'So why not do it?' I shouted,
But you were already on your way out.

8.

Drifts of dust in the corners,
poodles of fluff yapping.
The house was choking up and I couldn't clean.
Something was missing –
a woman's nature perhaps.
Somehow, in the womb, the Lord had forgotten to
        supply me
with a duster and brush.
I was born with a tongue in my head.

9.

A lot has dropped through the crack in the floor.
What we forgot is beginning to sprout.
Persephone's pomegranate has split its skin
and there in the midst of the furniture is rising
an amazing mirage.
It's so real
there are parrots in the trees
and we have to listen to an incessant
cockatooing

if you don't
if you could
if just sometimes

10.

Nettles infested the corners,
burdock clung to the lintel,
the home was weedy as Eden.
I knew there was a snake somewhere
and it was waiting its chance.

I yoo-hooed from room to room.
No one replied. There was only
a fly knocking its head on the window,
and the dust floating down in a cone of light
like plankton in a laboratory flask.

11.

Still, sometimes, at the gateway of a kiss
and the entrance of night a light scintillates –
wonder, tenderness.
We dive deep into each other
carried by feeling.
At the daring moment of night
when there's time enough to waste
our sides touch the unconceived.
It's blind and speechless.

12.

Nature scared us, we didn't know
which eggs it grew
birds in,
which reptiles.
We were cagey,
sitting on stones supposed to hatch,
our egg a last will and testament.

Suddenly it burst open like a hot oven.
Incredible.
We lay mangled
under a pile of unrealised possibilities.

How do you say adieu to dead like these? –
a dragon
with three heads poised for a fight;
a firebird
burnt to a frazzle in its shell.

13.

I found the snake:
my jaw has a wisdom tooth in
that oozes venom –
gloomy balloons in the comic strip of my life.
Its roots reach back to childhood.
(There were three to hate, three
I had to share everything with; finally
this became love, the sharing.)

When I'd shed my baby-teeth
and forgotten childhood
(so unimportant)
I fell passionately in love
in the way one can with
a person one hates deeply enough.

I didn't remember how deep the roots were:
the tough ligaments of helplessness, longing and jealousy.

14.

For a moment I dreamt
we'd kiss
till our teeth fell out!
We'd begin from the beginning –
like the unweened.

Impossible!
who'd look after us?

EURYDICE

Jana Štroblová
translated by Ewald Osers

From the faint flickering flames of memories
beyond the river of oblivion
(from the soul's underworld)
led out into the light. By day.
He (oh, that roguish smile!)
would even
rob Charon of his coin. Now he made you
walk
blindfold (What is? And what is not?)
with him, behind him…

Pity – he no longer looks back!

But you are in the light,
once more in this life!

THE STORY OF THE EXECUTIONER, THE VICTIM AND THE SPECTATOR

Mette Thorsen
translated by Anne Born

A IS plagued by reluctant rage when he is confronted with something unfathomable. He gives it a cracking good hiding. He wouldn't be able to say which of them is a cold, lead-coloured lump that refuses to budge. If the unfathomable were to reciprocate the hiding it would hear a thin, tinny sound, if it tasted him he would taste of tin can.

His rage bears no resemblance to the zestful reluctance he used to boil over with when he came into contact with another will. He would fire off one thought there, leap into the next one here, in a long crackling self-ignition, released by the friction. It is so long ago that the recollection is at the far rim of his memory, and the next attempt to remember will topple it over the edge.

But now it seems as if he and the unfathomable will have to chafe against each other until Judgement Day. The more he rubs, the more the sandpapery surface of the unfathomable spreads, until it covers each fold and fibre of him. Not a spot can escape. He tries to help himself by shrinking up into a little grey pea, which has the misfortune of having an inbuilt gravity that prevents it from rolling away.

The unfathomable has kneeled down and is mumbling discordant consonants and vowels. Why is it whimpering? Why is it secreting a liquid that smells of rotten eggs? If only it would stop. He has an axe he can use to make it stop.

Is A up to it?

When B was very young he sneaked a view of one of the executions that children were forbidden to watch. He never afterwards forgot the blend of held-back giggles and horror that had seized him. The victim had looked so comic, whimpering and trying to get away: like two pedestrians who come face to face on a pavement and can't agree which side of the other to go, executioner and victim shuffled backwards and forwards with the preliminary blows of the axe between them, until the executioner at one swoop released himself from the painful situation.

Ever since then B has lived in an aquatic world of slow dignified movements. He is the fattest man in town, because he hates the sudden ability of hunger to strike down and humiliate his guts, he avoids decisions that can't be deferred for a couple of years, and when he addresses his letters he writes out all the abbreviations in full.

One day he gets out of the bath without holding on to anything but a bar of soap, and both feet slide from under him so violently that he does the splits. He breaks both thigh bones and dislocates his hips. He can't get up and has almost lost the power of speech. But he sees the lavatory brush close to his hand, and if he knocks loudly enough on the pipe someone will hear and perhaps come to his aid. He can clearly hear the sound of passers by outside the window.

Is B up to it?

C sets great store on being able to react to danger. All round the clock his air alarm urges him to do fire practice, and he always looks away when anything is shown in slow motion on television.

One day he survived a competition, the challenge was to sail in a barrel through a famous labyrinth, composed of a many-branched sewer system, and the conditions were that if he lost he would receive a suitable penalty while if he succeeded in getting out at the other end he would get a large sum of money. In the afternoon he came to a village where there was to be an execution. The condemned man was granted the right to speak out for half an hour first. If C had been in his place he would have taken a deep breath and spoken for the half hour, breathing out, on:

the nature of murderers

on how they should be found out, unmasked, and disposed of through a revolution, he would have laid plans for the rest of the spectators' lives, bidden farewell to everyone he knew, even the most fleeting acquaintances, after that he would have taken hold of a fold of the executioner's tunic and felt the quality of the material, and tried the sharpness of the axe with his thumb: the final half hour would not have been distinguishable from the rest of his life, for it too would be marked by not being up to it. There isn't enough time. There isn't enough to meet the demand.

Meanwhile the condemned man wastes time. His last moments are worthless. He has found a way of taunting the executioner. His lips are tightly closed, nothing can pass them.

C has fallen into a trap which no speed can lift him out of: he sees the victim imprisoned in a trap from which no resolve can liberate him. It makes C's head ache.

Now it amuses the king to ask a volunteer from the spectators to toss up. If it's tails, the spectator will have to change places with the victim. If it's heads, the king must change places with the spectator.

Will C be up to it?

EVENING

Tom van Deel
translated by James Brockway

We were standing beside a lake and thinking
along with the water and the light,
which did not fade, for it was summer
and the far north. So finely poised
between leaving and everlastingness
there was nothing that could happen anymore
and everything seemed finally a fact.

NAMES

Tom van Deel
translated by James Brockway

When I'd one hundred and ninety different types
entered on cards, with number, place and date,
and sometimes with other details too,
like 'taken in flight', 'late evening', or 'with Ben',
I thought I'd got this world quite neatly taped:
What flew around my head had come to hand
in names: redshank, godwit, wren –
which meant exactly nothing in the end.

AT THE MONASTERY OF ST. BARNABAS

Zdeněk Vaníček
translated by Ewald Osers

In the midday heat
when even the walls blister
amidst the May drought
a soft distant whisper

a few swallows rising
a field bare in the morning
the whispering voices
are a final warning

THE OLD JEWISH QUARTER
IN PRAGUE

Zdeněk Vaníček
translated by Ewald Osers

for Ivan Jelínek

Pain here has dug up every corner
through the Street 'By the Old School' a hearse is moving
the house 'The Three Musketeers' jealously guards
     a single tree
between the river and the Astronomical Clock
absent-minded crowds are milling
in the collapsed ant-heap
crushed underfoot by Broad Street

Under Ota Janeček's windows
in the Old Jewish Cemetery with Rabbi Löw's tomb
in the dust of the Golem
(and of centuries)
ravens are croaking

Around the Merciful
in the shade of the Holy Ghost
and the Old-New Synagogue
dust is rising

Behind the hearse
a piano tinkles from an open window
and the potter's wheel starts spinning
a new cycle of birth
its magical *shem*

MY FATHER
THE COUNTRY DOCTOR

Guntram Vesper
translated by Michael Hulse

Those dead nights that first winter
after the war he'd drive out, the roads
to the village had vanished
under the drifting snow.

If he got stuck in the car he'd take his shovel
and dig his way through to the nearest farmer.

Decades later I discovered
the missing driver and
the stripped car again, in
yesterday's photos
held out to me by a shaking hand
by way of explanation
for a whole life.

THE TRACK

Guntram Vesper
translated by Michael Hulse

Their contemptible stratagems
had rapidly become
exciting or amusing anecdotes
you were expected to gape
and not ask questions.

The way they cheated
the Jewish chemist who
lived on the market square
over the sale of that
beautiful elegant house.

When we shifted our things
from the shabby shop
to the chemist's
on a borrowed cart,
under all the junk
a tub of honey had tipped up
and dripped a sticky track
on the cobbles, dogs
came from all around

licking the street
clean behind us,
we laughed
and laughed.

IN A SMALL TOWN

Guntram Vesper
translated by Michael Hulse

They lived in the houses on the market square
the shops on the ground floor
their rooms upstairs
gardens at the back down to the river.

That was how life had begun and that
was how it went on.

In thirty-eight they led the girl
from the post office around the streets
with a notice slung round her neck

and five years later they helped
haul up the Polish lad
to the top

two days he hung
at first floor height.

CONTRIBUTORS

MARÍA VICTORIA ATENCIA was born in 1931 in Malaga. She has published twelve books of poetry, including *Arte y parte* (*Art and Part*, 1961) and *La Pared Contigua* (*The Adjoining Wall*, 1989), plus several anthologies.

ANNE BORN is a poet, historian and translator of Scandinavian languages. She has published six volumes of poetry and many translations, including poems by Bo Carpelan and Pia Tafdrup, as well as prose, including Karen Blixen's *Letters from Africa*, the film script of *Babette's Feast* and two novels by Helle Stangerup.

LOUIS BOURNE has lived in Spain for the last twenty-four years and is studying for a PhD. As well as his own poems his translations of Spanish poets have appeared in many magazines and anthologies, including *New Directions 30, Granite, Stand, International Poetry Review* and *Outposts*. His most recent book is *Contemporary Poetry from the Canary Islands* (Forest Books), edited by Sebastian Nuez Caballero (to be reviewed in the next issue of *Sunk Island Review*).

JAMES BROCKWAY has been publishing his translations of Dutch literature since 1947. He received the Martinus Nijhoffprijs for his services to Dutch literature in 1966. His poems, short stories and translations have appeared in *Iron, Stand, London Magazine* and many other magazines. Enitharmon recently published a book-length collection of his translations of Rutger Kopland, *A World Beyond Myself* (to be reviewed in the next issue of Sunk Island Review).

RICHARD CADDEL visited Estonia in September 1991 to give a series of readings and lectures. His most recent collection is *Uncertain Time* (Newcastle, 1991).

BO CARPELAN born in 1926, is one of Finland's most distinguished poets writing in Finland-Swedish. An academic librarian, he has published many collections of poetry. He is also a novelist, playwright, essayist and critic.

ADAM CZERNIAWSKI is a Polish poet and translator living in England. His most recent publications include *Jesien*, (Krakow, 1989), a book of poems, and *People on a Bridge*, (Forest Books, 1990). Serpent's Tale published his autobiography, *A Disturbed Childhood*, in 1991. During 1991 he was Translator in Residence at the British Centre for Literary Translation at the University of East Anglia.

JEAN DAIVE was born in 1941 and lives in Paris. In 1970 he founded the review, *Fragment*. A number of collections of his poetry have appeared, including *Décimale Blanche* (1967) and *Narration d'équilibre* (1990).

ANDRES EHIN was born in Tallinn in 1940. He is noted for his surrealism and quirky humour. For many years he was a prominent member of the Estonian independence movement. His selected poems are in *Taiskuukeskpaev* (*Full Moon at Midday*).

GABRIEL FERRATER (1922-1972) was the finest of the Catalonian poets to emerge in the 1950s. He was also known as a linguist, a translator and a critic of art and poetry. His collected poems, *Les dones i els dies* (*Women and Days*) were published in 1968 and have been reprinted many times.

UNDINE GRUENTER was born in 1952. She studied Law, Literature and Philosophy at Heidelberg, Bonn and Wuppertal and now lives in Paris. She has published two novels (*Ein Bild der Unruhe*, 1986 and *Vertreibung aus dem Labyrinth*, 1992) and two collections of stories (*Nachtblind*, 1989 and *Das Gläserne Café*, 1991).

VÁCLAV HAVEL Essayist, playwright, author, Ex-President of the Ex-Czechoslovak Republic. The piece printed here is included in his recent book, *Letní Premitani*, and was first published in the *New York Review of Books*.

JOSÉ HIERRO was born in Madrid in 1922. He was imprisoned for over four years at the age of seventeen accused of helping Spanish Civil War prisoners. He was a founding editor of the poetry magazine *Proel*. He has published eight books, including *Libro de las hallucinationes* (*Book of Hallucinations*, 1964) and *Agenda* (1991). He has received the Adonais, National, Critics' and Principe de Asturias Prizes.

MICHAEL HULSE was born in Stoke-on-Trent in 1955 of Anglo-German parentage. His poems, reviews and translations have appeared in many places (including volumes by Penguin and Serpent's Tail) and he has won a number of prizes, including an E. C. Gregory Award and the Cholmondeley Award. He lives in Cologne, where he is a part-time lecturer at the University, and he is also Director of the Cologne International Literature Festival. His own most recent collection is *Eating Strawberries in the Necropolis* (Harvill, 1991)

MIRELA IVANOVA was born in 1962 in Sofia. She graduated from Plovdiv University in Bulgarian and Russian Languages and Literatures and now works on a literary periodical. Together with Boyko Lambovski, another Bulgarian poet, she founded 'Friday the Thirteenth', a group of poets rebelling against the stereotyped poetry culture under the communist regime. She is the author of four collections and some literary criticism.

PHILIPPE JACCOTTET was born in Moudon, Switzerland in 1925. He studied at the University of Lausanne. In 1946 he went to Paris as a representative of the Swiss publishers, Mermod. He was a regular contributor to *Nouvelle Revue Française*. He now lives in the Drôme. Various collection of his poems have been published, including *Requiem* (1947) and *Leçons* (1969).

CLARA JANÉS born in Barcelona in 1942, has degrees in Liberal Arts and Comparative Literature from the Universities of Pamplona and Paris respectively. Among her twelve books of poetry are *Eros*, (1981) and *Creciente Fértil* (*Fertile Crescent*, 1989). She has also published two novels, the better-known being *Los caballos del sueño* (*The Horses of Dream*), and translated work by a number of European writers, including Holan, Seifert, Duras, Sarraute, Mansfield and William Golding.

MARTTI JOENPOLVI was born on the shore of Lake Ladoga in Finland (the Karelia region) in 1936. Since 1945 he has lived in Tampere. He has published eighteen novels and short story collections since 1959.

OLE KORNELIUSSEN was born in Nanortalik, Greenland, in 1947. He studied Medicine at Copenhagen University. His first book, *Putog*, was a collection of poems published in 1973, reprinted when a collection of stories came out in 1991. He was awarded a Greenland Government grant for 1990-91.

KRISTOFFER LEANDOER was born in Stockholm in 1962. He studied Art and Literature at the University of Stockholm. At various times in his life he has been a hospital orderly, a secondhand bookseller, a journalist and a theatre critic. He has worked for *Dagens Nyheter*, Sweden's largest morning paper, and has published three collections of poetry, including *Stjärngräs* (*Stargrass*, 1991).

RIA LEIGH-LOOHUIZEN was born in Haarlem and has lived in Spain and the USA. She has translated the work of many Dutch poets into English. At present she is preparing an anthology, *Ten Dutch Individualists*, as well as a volume of poetry by Ed Leeflang.

HERBERT LOMAS has been a lecturer at the Universities of Helsinki and London, is a regular critic for the *London Magazine* and has published eight books, the most recent being *Letters in the Dark* (OUP, 1986) and *Contemporary Finnish Poetry* (Bloodaxe, 1991).

BRONISŁAW MAJ was born in 1953 in Lodz. He studied Polish Language and Literature at the Jagiellonian University in Krakow and co-edited the influential magazine, *Student*. He has published five collections of poetry. Translations of his work have appeared in magazines and journals around the world. Under martial law Maj circumvented censorship by running a popular literary monthly, *Na Glos* (*Speaking Out*), which was awarded an honorary prize by Solidarity. The magazine now continues under his editorship in normal printed form.

JOYCE MANSOUR was born in Bowden, England in 1928 of Egyptian parents. she spent most of her early life in Egypt before settling in Paris. She contributed a great deal to Surrealist reviews such as *Le Surréalisme même* and *La Breche*. Her collections include *Cris* (1954) and *Faire signe au machiniste* (1977). She died in 1986.

ADRIAAN MORRIEN born in Ijmuiden in 1912, is a poet, prose writer, essayist, critic and translator. He has edited several literary magazines and was a member of the celebrated Gruppe '47 which included Günter Grass and Heinrich Böll. His most recent publication is a collection of autobiographical stories and notes.

EWALD OSERS was born in Prague in 1917 and has lived in England since 1938. He has translated over 110 books and hundreds of his translations of poetry have appeared in magazines and anthologies all over the world. A collection of his own poetry, *Wish You Were Here*, was published in 1976, and another, in Czech translation, *Anamnéza*, appeared in Prague in 1986. He has won several translation prizes and has been awarded numerous honours, including an Honorary PhD and the German Order of Merit.

BLAS DE OTERO was born in Bilbao in 1916 and died in Madrid in 1979. He earned degrees in Law and Liberal Arts, taught in Bilbao and lived as a writer in Madrid. He published some eleven books of poetry and several anthologies, including *Ángel fieramente humano* (*Fiercely Human Angel*, 1950) and *Que trata de España* (*Speaking of Spain*, 1964).

CONSTANTY PUZYNA (1929-1989) was a prominent Polish theatre critic and Editor of the respected drama monthly, *Dialog*. His poetic output is confined to a slim volume published shortly before his death.

CLAUDIO RODRÍGUEZ born in Zamora in 1934, received his degree in Romance Languages from Madrid's Complutense University, and lectured from 1958 to 1964 at the Universities of Nottingham and Cambridge. He has published five books, including *Conjuros* (*Spells*, 1958) and *Casi una leyenda* (*Almost a Legend*, 1991). He has received the Adonais, Critics and National Prizes and was recently made a member of the Spanish Royal Academy.

MARTIN SORRELL is Lecturer in French at the University of Exeter, a post he has held since 1970. He studied French and spanish at Oxford and Kent. He has translated many French authors and won a prize in the British Comparative Literature Association's Translations competition in 1983.

EIRA STENBERG born in Tampere 1942, studied piano at the Sibelius Academy. She is a freelance writer. Her publications include *Parrakas madonna* (*Bearded Madonna,* 1983) and a selection of translated work in *Contemporary Finnish Poetry* (Bloodaxe, 1991, edited by Herbert Lomas).

JANA ŠTROBLOVÁ was born in Prague in 1936. Before the Soviet invasion of Czechoslovakia in 1968 she had published four books of poetry. After the invasion she was forced to leave her work as an editor of children's literature and was unable to publish for the next ten years. During the 1970s she did translation work under an assumed name. She runs poetry programmes on Prague Radio and is Vice-Chair of the Czech PEN.

ARTHUR TERRY was born in York in 1927 and is currently a Professor of Literature at the University of Essex. He has written numerous books and articles on Spanish, Catalan and Latin American literature and his collected essays on modern Catalan poetry were recently published by Ediciones 62, Barcelona. He is an active translator of modern Spanish and Catalan poetry and is currently working on a selection of poems by José Ángel Valente.

METTE THORSEN was born in 1957. At present she is a student in Copenhagen.

TOM VAN DEEL was born in Holland in 1945. His fourth collection, *Achter der Waterval* (*Behind the Waterfall*), was published in 1984.

ZDENĚK VANÍČEK only started writing a few years ago. He is a painter and has exhibited in Czechoslovakia and abroad. After a distinguished career as a diplomat (First Secretary in London, subsequently Head of the Western Europe Department in the Czechoslovak Ministry of Foreign Affairs, part of Václav Havel's entourage), he left the service to devote himself to painting, poetry and the organisation of international cultural events.

GUNTRAM VESPER was born in Frohburg in 1941 and studied in West Germany at the University of Giessen, in recent years spending his time in Göttingen. He has written poetry, prose and radio plays. His book, *Die Inseln im Landmeer* (*Islands in the Sea of Land*, 1982) won the Peter Huchel Prize.

PAUL WILSON is a translator living in Toronto. He has been translating Havel's recent speeches.